The Process of Intuition

Cover art by *Jane A. Evans*

The Process of Intuition

VIRGINIA BURDEN TOWER

*This publication made possible with
the assistance of the Kern Foundation*

The Theosophical Publishing House
Wheaton, Ill. U.S.A.
Madras, India/London, England

The Theosophical Publishing House
306 West Geneva Road
Wheaton, IL 60187

A publication of the Theosophical Publishing House, a department of the Theosophical Society in America.

Library of Congress Cataloging in Publication Data

Tower, Virginia Burden.
  The process of intuition.

  (A Quest book)
  1. Intuition (Psychology)   I. Title.
BF311.T67   1987   131   87-40128
ISBN 0-8356-0622-8 (pbk.)

To those who were with me
when the need was the greatest

CONTENTS

Preface to the Second Quest Edition

WHEN I considered this book in terms of a new edition, certain things struck me. The thesis has borne the weight of years of practical application. It maps out a kind of blueprint for the reconstruction of a life. This is evident if one looks into it seriously. It also becomes very clear that "the process" is necessarily played out in the psychological nature of the individual inquirer. As the confusion and conflicts of the "I" are addressed, there is room for something new to take place.

I feel that the insights I recorded in the book were and are valid. I would express some things differently now. The tone of the writing would be altered in places—would reflect the changes in myself wrought by time and maturation. For this reason I have added a chapter at the end entitled "The Traveler in Winter." It focuses on the perspective of my senior years, and it remains to be seen whether or not it will flesh out some of the mysteries of "the process." Life events in and of themselves are of relative importance. They only become important when utilized to activate the dynamics of change.

I would like to call attention to one aspect of this study of intuition which is implicit in my writing, but which ought to have been clearly brought out. Intuition opens a doorway to many kinds of knowledge. Unfortunately, the histories of gifted people show clearly that it is as often used for unwholesome purposes as for good. Or it may have worked positively in the beginning, but when one places oneself under fire from the cathartic forces that are aroused by the aspirant's own zeal, all too often pride and ambition take over. When this happens, subtle forms of aberration occur in the attitude and behavior of the individual, and his gift ultimately becomes a menace to himself and to others.

I do not mean to frighten readers away from encouraging "the process." Given a degree of self-honesty and a sense of genuine urgency about the need for change, there is always the prospect of increased awareness.

Preface to Quest Edition

A Thing in Motion

In That strange state of consciousness when the heart is reaching and thought has frayed out to thin, unimportant stuff without any form, a shutter of the soul sometimes springs open and fixes an image for an instant. The image itself may be trivial, but it palpitates with meaning for the life of the meditator.

There is a particular image that often comes to me in this way. It is the composite of a story I once read by Kipling about a terrible place where it was the cruel and superstitious custom to dump dying citizens into a great crater surrounded by slippery sands that wouldn't permit them to climb back to life, should they refuse to die properly and as predicted. Some lived on and eked out an existence from a source of water, from scraps of food thrown to them, and from crows they snared.

It's a sordid story, yet the image doesn't present itself to my intuitions in that light. My intuitions are saying something infinitely hopeful to me, infinitely sweet and suggestive. They are saying, "These are the half-dead, and you, also, are of the half-dead. The trick is to die a little more and all will be well." And how I want to "die" in the sense that my intuitions instruct me!

The self, at last, is to be studied and known in the Socratic sense only so that it can be eliminated. This is my excuse for using my reflections as thesis material. I long to dispose of myself. Hopefully, the end product of my meditations will be something like Michelangelo's caricature of himself in his mural, "The Last Judgement" . . . an empty sack of a thing pulled up out of the chastening purgatorial stew.

What is this death that I strain toward? Surely it has nothing to do with that hoped-for oblivion or, at the least, a transfer from one locale (now grown intolerable) to another which prompts the widespread "death wish" that is in the air these days. From living too fully and freely, it seems one uses up life quickly and starts to contemplate death too soon. This is one view of the matter.

Some of our ancestors had a different view of life and death. They used life very cautiously and circumspectly, like a not-too-congenial obligation that one performs with a slightly averted face. Their eyes were focused elsewhere. They regarded human occupations as the means by which the soul is forged, and the substance of the soul had to be gathered drop by precious drop, the distillate of living and trying. The modern world changed the process radically. Now one chooses experience, like wines from a shelf, to invigorate the very part of man's nature that our ancestors considered expendable—the sludge at the bottom of the crucible.

Perhaps our ancestors caught the hemline of a truth as it skirted away from them. A handful of finely-wrought stuff was enough to give a pale color to their best earthly ambitions and pleasures and to make them disparaging about life. One suspects, though, that they missed the point that the good death could only be fabricated from the well-loved life and when they did, in fact, die, it is possible that their Heaven turned out to be depressingly familiar.

But let us suppose a unique kind of person with an exceptional mind who regards death and life as a joint phenomenon and who seeks to effect the whole wonder within his own psychological nature. He might, in the process, develop un-common capacities. Then, as like attracts like, he might gravitate in sympathy toward his own kind; for this is the way of any new species. I think that such entities exist; and if they do not form geographical communities, they do form what might be called "thought communities." And must they be corporeally "dead" or even "alive" for that matter? If these two clumsy terms—parts of a continuous experience—must be reckoned with, are they not, in the present case, somewhat irrelevant?

However, induction into this new communal state cannot be an easy thing to accomplish. One does not metamorphose from one species to another overnight. No, there must be an arduous interval, whatever its length, and it must seem very long psychologically whatever its duration in fact. To probe the contents of that interval, one must strike at a midway language between the two states. The intuition has to milk the ether of its instruction, to process it with whatever poor words lie ready at the mind's disposal and, in the end, sigh over the disparity between the insight and the little splash of words which, once fallen from their high place to the hard ground of the intellect, begin to lose their precious life substance.

From time to time, I have peeked into myself like an eager magician, trying to hurry along an exciting and difficult process. On each occasion I have come away with the hard-to-live-with conclusion that I'm neither fish nor fowl. In fact, the state of man generally is not unlike that of a fish confined to the resistance of the heavy medium of water as contrasted with the lighter medium of air.

The biologist suggests that there is a time in the life cycle of a water creature when he makes his terrible effort to move to land, and one can imagine him stumping along on his broken fins and the distress of that first breath drawn more from prophecy than from common sense; and yet one may suppose a kind of propulsion of the spirit that yearned so joyously toward the new state that the creature hardly felt the parts and pieces of himself being dropped along the way.

The death-in-life is analogous in some ways. The soul, being ready, summons up the sensitive, outward-reaching spearhead of the waking consciousness, and it surges forward in answer to the summons, trailing much of itself behind. The more progress that is made, the greater is the attenuation until a definition becomes absurd. If I were to pose the perennial philosophical question, "What am I?" I would have to answer, "I am a thing in motion." Outwardly, I have never quite shaken the semblance of a middle-class school teacher with a flare for the theatrical, a carry-over from my amateur play-acting days. Inwardly . . . ah! . . . inwardly I am something quite different.

I'm reasonably comfortable where I sit—the unblushing armchair philosopher taking the journey through the passage that connects life and death in an indistinguishable continuity. Along the way I made some notes. The impulse came from an instinct about the laws surrounding my adventure and not from any notion of doing good. At the periphery of my vision, I see that some good may come of it, but this is not my first concern. I am, as I should be, too busy and amazed and altogether enthused with my adventure to think about that.

But those laws! . . . Those awesome laws of nature! They rise up in one's path like the very sinews of the Universe that bind and control all of the rest. One learns early to make deferential accommodation to them. At times they catch the unwary traveler and nearly yank him out of his place; but at other times—along one of the dark and forbidding byways of which there are many—they are an Ariadne's thread leading through the labyrinth. So I made notes, sketchy and unsatisfactory as they are likely to seem. I called them, "The Process of Intuition."

I suppose there is some wisdom—difficult as it is to imagine—in requiring an infant who is not even free of the birth canal to record its impressions; but then philosophy must be anchored to human lives or where are we? It is a frustration to read the terse aphorisms of the wise, which they usually offer up at the end of extraordinary lives in a receptacle small as a Chinese teacup, with nothing of the boil of the adventure to tell us how and whence they came. Should we try these quaint sayings on for ourselves—we whose lives are so foreign to all of that? And so there is the impassable gulf between the fine sentiments aroused in the mind and heart by such sayings and, dividing us from those sentiments, the action which produced them. Is not this the dilemma of religion and its failure?

I believe that the spiritual darkness that swarms over today's world remains for want of a first step, a first actual stirring from one's position before the fixed doors of one's abode. The yearnings, hopes, follies, prayers, and passions of the ordinary everyday self are the primordial substance from which a new life may spring. All it wants is a certain juxtaposition of elements and—behold!

So it became my task to try to take a reading and more or less chart my position; then to try to trace a little of the route and the means by which I had arrived thus far. The ink hardly dried upon the paper before I was in motion again and the record thrown slightly askew thereby. No matter! The effect of my effort gave a little momentum to me and to others, so I let the record stand.

Although the weather is never really placid or my vehicle wholly dependable, there is just now a good sense of well-being and equilibrium. I am still in the passage but there are nautical extensions of vision. I seem to be provided with sharper and more far-seeing instruments as I move along. There is a keener balance between vehicle and elements—a coming to terms each with the other. The furies are appeased, and I am content to be "a thing in motion."

Introduction

DIGNITY AND DISASTER

If our nuclear age requires that we perch precariously on the brink of disaster for an indefinite number of years, then we must find a position that will contain the tension and ensure human dignity. The man of spiritual fiber does not so much dread the thought of death as he dreads that moment which so startles and disorients him that he loses his seat in the Universe. His only worry is that the sum of his content may prove so trifling and so feeble a brew that life's biggest trial will find him wanting—forgetful of the grand vision, the humming reality.

If our pathetic political contrivings will somehow permit us to live, let us not lose the advantage that the state of alarm lends to the soul. Let us use it for noble purposes. Fear is astringent to apathy, uncertainty juggles convictions, and despair has its own strange renewal force.

What is this life we covet and guard so jealously? It is most often a thing of duration and not of substance. To endure is pointless if endurance is mere prolongation of inanities, with small excitements and petty triumphs the only reward for the dullness of our everyday lives. Duration without substance is an idiot's existence. Why so fearsome the bombs, then? The horror has been and is. It is the horror we must end. It is the life of significance we must begin, and a small quantity, even, of such a life can justify existence. Each moment of insight quickens the slumbering inner life into activity, and, however feeble, reverberates throughout the universe. Each adds a small portion to our pitiful store. But small as it may be, it is this quantity which enfranchises us against spiritual oblivion.

So, if by no other means we can rise to full stature, we can meet the tide of destruction in our own natures. This is where it originated, before it fused and grew into the proportions of war. If only through threatened chaos can we summon our long-neglected spiritual reserves, then let us greet the threat. No bomb can kill a man who is already dead; he must first come alive.

What, again, is this threatened mortal destruction? A flotsam horde pursuing a jetsam multitude! Quantity is not impressive when the constituents are nil. A thing must be intrinsically valuable to be threatened. The savages warred over the commodities of their times—shells, feathers, and injured pride. What do we find so valuable among our own possessions and attributes that we can dignify its possible loss by applying the term "threatened"? Things of enduring value are not stored in or on the land nor placed for the convenience and pleasure of mankind. Things of enduring value are found, spare and precious, in the hearts of a few who are extraordinarily brave and sagaciously intelligent. And —although such a brave and sagacious man may be threatened from without—only, at last, can his own self-inflicted gesture destroy his substance. He may, under duress from within or without, bury, as though with bombs, his own treasure. No other agency can touch it. Or he may add to his quantity and build himself into the eternal fabric of the Grand Design.

But what if no such substance exists in the heart of man? Then he contrives foolishly when he seeks to save himself. He must first come alive. This is not a question of time or circumstances, though a severe challenge is serviceable for his pur-

pose. It is a question of insight and necessity. Our very indus-
try is a procrastination, for boredom and nervous fatigue seem
preferable to the pain of deep psychological change and uncertainty. One must look deeply, sternly at oneself and the
facts of our way of life. One must cease to inflate the value of
one's familiar duties and occupations, to pose them as a
justification for inconsequential choices and actions. An inspired man can fulfill the normal duties of life with his left
hand and use his right for thrusting and probing after
realities.

But our short-sighted problems teach us petty virtues. We
lack the discernment, even, to notice the great and worthy
trials that arise in the life of one who aspires. The magnitude
of such trials can rack a man to awareness or dissolution.
There are those—a few—who consider this a proper kind of
battle for a human being. Because it is so vastly different in
quality and implication from the absurd battles between na-
tions, it smothers them in the lofty contempt of a timeless
perspective. What is this piddling mortal nature that you, the
twentieth century, threaten with maiming and extinction? If I
myself value it hardly at all, feeling its littleness as compared
with the grand purport of my clarity and dignity, then how
shall you threaten me? I am busy on my own front lines and
trenches, a "No Man's Land" of which you have no inkling!

Often it is reported that when a person thinks he is going to
die, his consuming feeling is one of disappointment over
failure of accomplishment. In the intuitive moment that
comes during the supreme crisis, he feels like a man sent on
an important errand who has tarried so long on the way that
he fails to accomplish the one task for which he was sent.
Probably—whether we die in a nuclear war or live out a
normal span of life—the majority of us will experience a
similar disappointment when the last hour comes. If we
would have it otherwise, then let us yield to the symptoms
that the threatening world crisis evokes in our minds and
bodies. Let us feel thoroughly alarmed, agonizingly sensitive,
painfully tentative and uncertain, and full of the conviction of
necessity. It is in such a condition that a man ripe for insight
finds himself—war or no war.

Man may, if he has the caliber, perch on the brink of disaster and turn his circumstances to the benefit of himself and mankind. Only an enlightened man—a man of secure substance—can speak hopefully of the things we all long for: freedom, wisdom, charity, and happiness. Such a man is indestructible, for all that he treasures in himself is immortal.

1. SUMMONS TO SURVIVAL

THERE is a sad, silent and very painful struggle going on under the surface of our society which threatens to form a mortal cleavage between two kinds of people. These two kinds of people may be designated as the *intellectual* and the *intuitive*. Many and varied are the states of consciousness between, and no one falls purely into one class or the other; yet in this book the attempt is made to reduce metaphysical complexities to a framework of intelligible assertions which have practical meaning for every earnest inquirer.

Thinking people are generally aware that in our century, materialism and intellectualism—with its spur from the science laboratory—have become a threat to organized religion. In spite of church-attendance statistics, private opinion on religion is confused and embarrassed. In intellectual groups, it is tacitly agreed to avoid the subject, for there is no satisfactory intellectual approach to it. We also see that the impulse to find the meaning of life has gradually been finding outlet through metaphysical and psychical organizations of one kind and another. Sometimes openly, sometimes furtively, those people tend to gravitate toward one another who have the peculiar characteristic in common of being interested in that which lies beyond the normal range of perception. Together, they present a fact in evolution—that fact being the presence of a growing psychic condition in man. It is with us, this perception. Many people have experience of it, and it must eventually be reckoned with by even the most conservative element. A society that does not credit the abundant evidence of psychic and intuitional observation (the latter term will presently be explored at length) must suffer a slow and subtle disintegration.

Throughout the discussion, certain assertions will be made based upon an intensive practical inquiry into the subject. It is not possible to explain the *raison d'être* of every assertion, but it is hoped that the reader will let each stand tentatively and read on. Eventually, if he is so inclined, the whole will come together and demonstrate its own relatedness.

To begin with, then, mankind is evolving not only biologically, but in awareness as well. It is proceeding upward from the instinctual level to the intellectual and hence, to the intuitional level, these being what might be called "grades" of consciousness, though not clear-cut. Surrounding each of these levels are the attributes of that "grade" of man—the objects which he sets up as worthy of acquirement, the values he places on all things material, mental and moral.

Our present-day world is certainly largely dominated by intellect. We are fond of books and authorities, tests and calculations, debate and logic, and the accumulated evidence of statistics. Formal education is greatly sought after and highly esteemed. Science is for many the ultimate authority. The simple insight of the peasant is regarded as ignorance, and it is no longer true that we would welcome an illiterate man into our public offices or take his opinions seriously at our council tables. However, somehow, if we are to arrive at the intuitional level (assuming it is desirable to do so) we must reach down and rediscover our forgotten instincts and draw them up through the intellect to form the groundwork for intuitional ripening. Instinct without intellect is not serviceable. Too often it is haphazard and immoderate, claiming too much for itself.

That is why the attributes of mind found among intellectuals are so necessary for an orderly and mature approach to our subject. But unfortunately, in addition to the dignity and levelheadedness which the intellectual brings to a new concept, he brings also a large portion of skepticism and an unwarranted regard for the validity of the reasoning process. However deeply the intuitionist may yearn to communicate with the intellectual, the two constantly bypass one another, for the points of reference and the areas of relevancy for each exist on two separate planes of consciousness. It would appear that the "membrane" that divides intellect from intuition is so tough as to be almost impenetrable. Yet there are those whose minds are occasionally surprised by a freshet of meaning that seems to have found an opening in the tightly fixed mechanisms of logic and deduction. The warmth and ease of genius briefly flood the aching efforts of the mind, and henceforth the individual is less complacent, more pliable and better prepared for the extremely subtle areas of communication and relationship which are shared by intuitive people. To such as these, it is possible to speak without apology for the limitations of words, which invariably belabor what is in truth simple.

How far from our intention is it to give the impression that the intuitionist is all-wise and a good fellow to have on one's consulting list! If he is genuine, the intuitionist will be the last one to give personal advice. He is himself the student in the fullest sense of the word, for he has gone through a breakdown process that has bled most of the complacency out of him. But he has learned something of the method of wisdom, and in this respect alone he is in an advantageous position. Intuition, then, is not all-knowledge; it is, rather, a key to pertinent knowledge. How important it is to understand this! The tendency is to assume that we are all born empty and that life is a process of filling up with knowledge—always keeping, if possible, a little ahead of the rest. This results in the necessity for the reading of countless books and periodicals, of attending lectures, cultivating authorities, studying political and sociological trends, etc., etc. It is a nerve-racking skirmish which no one can hope to win. How much of this accumulated information is relevant to the basic issues of life is surely questionable. Also, in understanding the self and the peculiarly personal and individual direction of its evolution, function and contribution, we find that even less of the accumulation is relevant.

No, the intuitionist is not all-wise. He is merely an extremely flexible organism who feels his own strange destiny keenly, and who has discovered that he effortlessly attracts to himself the means to his own wisdom-needs. He is not in a mad pursuit after knowledge; he deliberately submits himself to a dynamic process of judicious selection. He learns that wisdom and unfoldment occur in the same atmosphere with the principle of cooperation. He becomes very teachable. He learns from everybody and everything, however humble. He knows that a very illiterate individual will have more to say to him sometimes than the most scholarly professor. He will see that animals, plants and children have much to give. Thus, he becomes wise in the sense of understanding principles, while blissfully steering clear of everything that does not concern him. Awareness changes throughout a lifetime, and with it, our values and proportions. Capacity, as a concept, gives way to relevancy.

In this process of attracting pertinent knowledge, one catches a glimpse of a principle that occurs over and over again in the wake of intuition. It is the fact that when we let go of the grip we have on things by virtue of our training and experience, we at once find ourselves in a field of automatic action. We are creatures caught under the sea, remaining rooted to the same position until there comes a growing sense of the validity and trustworthiness of the currents of influence that continually swirl about us. In the brief aftermath of letting go, one may imagine a certain feeling of disorientation and absence of perspective. But this passes, and the currents waft us swiftly off into a brand new impetus whose purpose we soon come to understand.

Arriving at a new point of perspective, we are delighted and amazed at the "miracle" of our swift and automatic deliverance, and we must at once concede that something has occurred which was clear outside the province of ordinary intellect. If we had tried to plan such a coup, it never would have happened. We can only wonder and feel very humble in the face of the evidence of such an all-encompassing Intelligence. More and more we see this automatic action at work. We see it as the silent operator in the selection of our associates. Relationship directly takes on an entirely different meaning in the face of it, and automatic action is perceived as the very essence of cooperation. When we understand cooperation, then we have the basis for the highest kind of social order.

2. THE FIRST NEW SHOOTS

Efforts to describe in words the meaning, nature and function of intuition must fail simply because intuition must be understood *by* intuition. The best that any written work on the subject can do is to attempt to put the reader in the way of having an intuitive experience himself, or to arouse in him the memory of such. It can give him certain lead-strings which, if permitted to set up a chain reaction of involuntary induction, will lead to certain conglomerates of principles and these again to other, larger conglomerates. We cannot reason about this intuition very much, simply because the intuitive faculty is one which transcends reason and makes it obsolete as the final authority. Very soon, we find we talk it out of existence altogether, for all practical purposes.

If any interested person digs around long enough, he will discover that quite a lot has been said in various books on the subject of intuition. He will find a bit here and a bit there. He will discover it called by different names and approached from different angles. He may end up with quite a body of objective information, such as that intuition is somehow brought into being with the help of the "third eye"—an atrophied, invisible organ located at the center of the forehead. He may read that intuition comes from God. He may see in the numerous psychic manifestations and in his own psychic experiences, large or small, the evidence of spirituality or intuition. He may call his hunches, his first flash judgments of people that tend to bear out his exceptional prophetic insight, *intuition*. But when he has summed it all up, he actually knows very little about the subject, and even knowing about a subject is quite a different thing from direct experience. Nor has he succeeded in making an orderly experiment of this type of experience, so that it becomes a reliable and accepted part of his daily perceptions that is taken for granted as much as his sight or hearing. Only when he has made the enormous effort to bring this faculty into full play so that he counts on it as he counts on the sensation of the earth beneath his feet is he qualified to make any claims. Those who are willing to undergo the arduous self-training to achieve this state must necessarily be few. Yet all of us may, if we feel the importance of it, make some progress on this road.

Why is it important to bother with this faculty? Quite aside from the personal unfoldment that it offers—the increasing insight into vistas of wisdom not available to the intellect, and real wisdom tending always toward a state of peace and creativity—it becomes the obligation of everyone who understands the situation to help the whole of mankind over the hump of a necessary evolutionary step. Nature gives ample proof that when new forms and expressions are given to life, these must either struggle into perfection or fall into malformation which in turn breeds further malformation in a long series of evils prior to extinction. The eternal impetus of nature is to move on, and almost all personal and social disruption results from the effort of individuals and societies to stand still—to plant themselves firmly against the current of intended progress and refinement.

It has been pointed out that the faculty is with us in its incipiency. It is a fact in our midst, and we must either help it into full and perfect fruition, or suffer as a societyy for our blindness and unwillingness to take a tangible fact out into the light and regard it with maturity and self-effacing honesty of observation. With the exception of a few groups and individuals who are trying to go at the subject with objective interest, this most serious subject has been left largely in the hands of instinctive, emotional people, who toy with it in all sorts of dangerous ways. Meanwhile, the majority of intellectuals are not aware that the crucial condition exists.

If it is true that the intuitive faculty exists and must find expression in the generations to come, then we must also see that other facts follow naturally upon the development of a new state of consciousness. Instinct has blended into and been swallowed up by intellect, and it is maintained that intellect in its turn (terrible as the idea may seem to some), must blend into and be swallowed up by intuition. In intuition, we find the synthesis and refinement of the two lower grades, and while intellect continues to have its function, it is in a wholly different order of precedence. Intellect becomes to the intuitionist as the hands to the brain. As in the beginning a child must laboriously count out by hand how many apples there are in the dish while the adult can see a dozen almost at a glance, so the intuition comes to supersede the usual process of reasoning things out. Intuition sees at a glance what might well take an ordinary mind a lifetime of trial and error to discover. Therefore, the very tendency to reason things out on the basis of experience and training must (horror of all horrors! thinks the rationalist) be quieted in order for intuition to come into play. The intellectual must tentatively (for in the beginning, he will never be convinced) put aside his esteemed instruments for perceiving, conceiving and evaluating in favor of the hypothesis that there is a far better, more inclusive and reliable way to observe and relate to life. *He must, in other words, let go of that which he already has in order to take up something new.* If you are carrying around a vessel with a leak in it, you must—if you discover the leak —set it down and go in search of another vessel. That you may in the meantime get a bit thirsty is conceivable and must be expected, but nature provides for her pupils during periods of transition, and if one is determined and sees the necessity for this new state of things, the bridge may be spanned between intellect and intuition, and by means that will often astonish the intellect.

But before one even attempts to start on a practical training program for developing the intuition (assuming such can be discovered) he must examine very carefully the matter of his goals. Almost everyone who enters into the various branches of occult research does so, consciously or unconsciously, for some form of personal gain. There is first of all the desire to outdistance the other fellow, to gain some skill or wisdom that will make one feel superior to others. There is the desire to lead others, to be an influence in their lives in order to chalk up a nice quota of virtue for oneself. Sometimes, most unfortunately, money enters into the picture. Certainly, very often the promise of "realizing" a far better way of life suggests itself, and this better way inevitably is predefined as one of affluent circumstances, security, prestige among one's fellows and all else that we have come to think of as valuable in our present-day society. Even the concept of peace is pre-defined as a state free of pressures of all kinds, in which one has only to lean back and clip the coupons miraculously manifested by a higher form of perception. Many metaphysical societies are propelled by this lure, and it is one which will inevitably lead to misery. The fact is, that to set up any goals at all for oneself, other than the most obvious interest in cooperating with the onward evolutionary trend, is waste and foolishness. You may think "What if I don't like the intuitive state after I arrive there?" That's a gamble one has to take and will take if one is sufficiently discontented. And whatever you think the intuitive state is, you will come nowhere near understanding it until you have actually approached it. You may be one of the few who sees the state of the world through the eyes of nature. You observe that the ground is melting away under the feet of the intellectuals, and that the misty outline of a virgin continent is opening up. You may see that the job of cultivation, of breaking land and bringing to order this new continent is not one that is a matter of choice at all, but one of necessity —unless one is so ostrich-like as to be entirely concerned with one's own puny span of life on this earth. It is not to the point to deal with possible rewards and opportunities in another life, for it is enough that future mankind needs some capable, interested pioneers right now. If one must think in terms of individual evolution, then there is a nice, all-inclusive principle to take into account: there is no future that has not been prefabricated in the immediate present. You are deciding right now what you will become a year from now or thereafter. If you were to be knocked unconscious and to remain that way for a year, when you awoke the world about you would have changed, but you would still have to make up for your absence. Most of us are very much "absent" in that we prefer to continue on year after year with the same opinions and beliefs regardless of what nature is doing.

Someone is sure to think that the best way to test the desirability of the intuitive way of life is just to find out all the details about some person who claims to live intuitively, and then to decide whether or not it suits his fancy. In the first place, the intellectual will never see the "fruits" gained by the intuitionist. He may find him struggling and disorganized in his personal life and fail to realize that there are two kinds of mess: the mess of deterioration and the mess of re-construction. He may find out some facts, but he will never know what is going on inside the other, or have any notion of the rationale which prompts his actions and the conditions in his life. Nor will he understand that in gaining intuition, one's goals and values alter so astonishingly that what was "sauce" for the intellect is "sour pickles" to the intuition. The most obvious lures lose their fascination, and the personal facts of his life actually mask the wondrous thing that is taking place. That there are rich rewards, new and subtle enjoyments, motivations of a wholly new order is a fact that can only be accepted on hearsay until one's development has proceeded far enough that he may discover for himself. But it is not these which should prompt the inquirer, but rather the state of necessity which was discussed. If he commences with a selfish motive, the very process will "twist in his hands," so to speak, and lead to all sorts of distressing consequences.

At this point, anyone who understands the subtle issues involved in what has been said will find himself at a crossroads where there is not very much time for pondering or beating about the bush. Nature points out a task to be accomplished on ourselves and suggests a hint of possible rewards. She also indicates that the way is uphill. Clearly there is no choice but to move on, reward or no reward, for any sane person wishes to do that which is inevitable anyway. It is simple expediency. *If, prompted by the spirit of expediency (for even curiosity is a sandtrap) and the unemotional desire to do the best that is possible in the interests of progress, one takes up the examination of intuition, he will make his discoveries in his own unique way with the required amount of safety.* There is absolutely no point in even contemplating the subject unless this motive is clearly realized.

3. EARLY GROWTH: SUN, SOIL, AND PREDATORY THREATS

IT IS going to be necessary to talk all around intuition—the actual state itself—and to suggest what it *is not*, something of the conditions under which it may be discovered, the kind of company it keeps, and the ways in which it may be manifest. Thus, knowing some of its properties and the environment which favors it, we may, by inference, give it some kind of reality. The tendency among intellectuals is to listen politely and then immediately ask you for your credentials, as though reason and perception could come into being only under the stimulus of accumulated data or established authorization.

The way of intuition is a direct perception of truth at its core, and to the one who sees an active principle in nature, there can be no more doubt than of the fact that the sun shines when we see it doing so with our own eyes and feel its heat upon our skin. Certainly the budding intuitionist is not omnipotent, but the principles which he does intuit without coloring from his intellect leave no shadow of a doubt simply because they are sensorially perceived. Reason is a process of selection—of comparison and discrimination resulting in a tentative choice. Sensory perception is a spontaneous and immediate acquaintance with the object under contact.

A visitor from England may tell you about the much-loved primrose—may describe in minute details its color, fragrance, shape, size, etc. He may show you some excellent photographs. He may even project some of his own subjective experience into his description, which you feel empathetically. If another party asks you if you know the primrose, you may say yes, you have some acquaintanceship with it. You may feel that you could not mistake the flower if you saw it; therefore, you *know* that flower. It is among those you could classify. Notwithstanding all your information and your capacity to assemble that information into a mental facsimile of the actual flower, you would surely know less qualitatively than the passing tourist who plucks one of the actual blossoms and holds it for an instant in his hands. It is in this way that the intuitionist comes into direct contact with a central body of principles which underlie the physical and mental phenomena which our intellectual world is constantly trying to calculate, analyze and tabulate through scientific method. Scientists are sincere, hard-working people, deserving of much credit in many instances, but we are—as a society—tracing out the bones, muscles and ligaments of the great body of phenomenal nature and ignoring the brain, which we might come to know intuitively and thus avoid the labor of a clumsy process that never seems to reach beyond the first joint.

It is contended that any sensitive, serious, intelligent person who is willing to lay aside his prejudice, training and experience in favor of the possibility of such a thing as intuition may experiment with it sufficiently to find his own proof. Intuition is like a latent talent for music that has been held in check for want of the proper conditions for its expression. But suppose a person with inherent musical genius is left alone with various instruments. He will only need to experiment in order to express that which is already in him. So it is with intuition; and although the "membrane" dividing intellect from intuition seems in some persons to be thinner than in others—a veritable virgin hymen ready for rupture and consequently the eventual process of birth—it is still often too overgrown, too desirous of maintaining its immature state to ever yield to the urge for spiritual maturation. Only those in whom insight is quickened to a necessary degree and the will to explore is so great as to outbalance every other consideration, is there any possibility of penetration. So we might conclude that intuition tends to flourish in an atmosphere of humility, intelligence and perseverance.

In all that has been said, little as it is, one must begin to connote the idea of a state of mind and heart rather than some sort of clever trick, like wiggling the ears or throwing the thumb out of joint. It has been suggested that certain ethical and moral considerations go along with intuition—the matter of motive and attitude. And such words as humility and intelligence have been employed. All of this should certainly suggest that we are dealing with something on quite a different level and of much more serious and far-reaching implications than purely objective phenomena. The words used —please note—have to do with subjective states. There are any number of highly intelligent, well-educated people who still believe that to master the hidden arts of nature, one needs only to practice certain mental and/or physical exercises. A taste of psychic phenomena and experience with hypnotism or other branches of similar experimentation inevitably lead to a great enthusiasm for these still mysterious matters.

Although such capacities as clairvoyance, psychic communication of various kinds, mind reading and prophesy may and actually do, at a certain stage, become tools for the use of the intuitionist, they are not in themselves a sign of active intuition. Because they are isolated and cut off from the philosophical rationale of the central body of truth, they are often extremely dangerous. While many sincere and honest people may start at one of these manifest extremities of the whole body and find their way to the "brain" itself, there are for each of these any number who will twist the big toe this way and that way until they earn for themselves a good swift kick in their most vulnerable region. Every person who submits to mediumship or hypnotism—who enters into séance circles, or assumes a state of trance—does so at an enormous risk to his health and sanity. With the full facts of nature herself as witness, it is urged that unless organizations for psychic experimentation have as their central purpose the desire to understand the moral atmosphere in which human understanding alone can flourish, these thrusts at the hidden psychic forces will have very harmful effects upon the psychic health of the subjects.

Certainly it is wise and good to look into the meaning and nature of sporadic phenomena wherever they present themselves; the danger comes from the infernal poking into the human mind under circumstances of absence of self-control and initiative. It ranks in the same category as the experimental efforts to probe the facts of mental abnormalities by use of the scalpel. Have we so little faith in nature that we fail to see that she has provided us with methods which do not require that we butcher and subjugate our brothers in an adolescent zeal to find out things? Why do we not get quiet long enough and take a deep enough look into our own natures to discover the simplicities, so that we do not fly in the face of the positive intent of nature? There is no evil which lacks an antidote, no problem for which an answer is not already proferred—so states intuition.

4. KINSHIP OF THE ONE WITH THE WHOLE

EXPERIMENTING with the use of intuition, one may safely assume that we are all parts of one Whole, and that this Whole knows each of its parts consecutively and spontaneously. Each of us is endowed with an attribute, principle or aspect of consciousness which may, with cultivation, be included in our everyday awareness, and which carries with it the accumulated content of the Whole. Not only does this Whole include people, but supposedly inanimate things as well, so that the permeation is complete.

When there is an intuitive impulse, one's entire body and being become a receiving set, and the density with which the mind is habitually shrouded separates over the hidden truth beneath for just an instant. That instant of tranquillity is like an interval when the movement of sea water on a rocky beach pauses and becomes lucid just long enough for the eye to catch the panorama of glistening shells and sea life upon the floor of the ocean. It is a strange and wonderful moment of clarity and conviction—this winking realization. Nor is this all of it, for intuition, being the perceiver of the source body of accumulated wisdom, sees not only the individual need, but the needs of the whole at one and the same time. It will never "do" for the individual that which is contrary to the general good.

Intuition, if we must label it—and in labeling it, let us not be deceived that we can approach the state itself through a label—is identification with a high order of intelligence intrinsic in nature and made available to man in a state of acute sensitivity. When we are rubbed raw by the difficult experiences of life—when we are pushed against the wall by acute sorrow, illness, shame or despair, we sometimes involuntarily escape through the hatch, as it were. With no other escape, we thrust directly through the center of the problem, and we have a brief experience of illumination. That such experiences can be encouraged into the normal flow of living is a fact that not many people seem to understand. If there is any time or room to reason a way out of our problems, we far prefer to do so, for the unfamiliar "shape" assumed in a moment of intuition is often distressing to an organism accustomed to certain habitual responses. Then too, we are likely to remember the painful circumstances that drove us out of our skins for a second, and think that it must always be so. But these are, nevertheless, moments of actual birth, when the grip of the brain and the flesh have slackened their hold for just a flash; and at the very moment when life itself seemed tottering and we no longer caring, lo and behold!—we find it is not all over, but rather, just beginning.

A faintly perceived, brand new entity comes into realization—the central figure in a new order of things. And as we observe the soundness, the infinite dependability of this new "voice," we come to trust it more and more, always relinquishing the tight hold of the intellect in order to make room for it. This intuitive source is unequivocally trustworthy; it is safe to assume that when fully developed in intuition, an individual becomes practically omniscient, though such individuals must surely be rare.

Given a truly sensitive individual, the process of life itself leads ultimately to intuitive experiences, as suggested above. The more keenly a person feels things, the more discontented he is, the chances are the more ripe he is for the development of intuition—assuming that he is not just a selfish malcontent, bent on his own pleasure. Then he need not continue to be tumbled and pressured by the currents of life, but may direct his will and observation in such a way as to cooperate with the intent of nature to open out his intuition, thus enormously increasing his understanding and usefulness.

Learning to trust one's intuition is something like learning to swim. The curious and mysterious fact is that we are all immersed in an invisible medium to which the intuitive person relates as the swimmer relates to water. In this medium, as in the ocean, there are currents, attractions, repulsions, vortices, proper rules of displacement and many other familiar properties, although the fact may be as hidden from the knowledge of the casual observer as the properties of water are hidden from the understanding of the landlubber. The key of access to this hidden knowledge consists of at least a spark of credulity (the spark itself cannot be there unless it arises from an intuitive source), a willingness to set aside beliefs and prejudices, and the will to face one's fear squarely. In this latter instance, the desire to overcome fear must actually be stronger than the desire to live. Impossible? There are those who have discovered that fear is death in life, and have willingly risked physical death and loss of all that is considered valuable in order to live in freedom.

But if one has enough control of his timidity—if he can hold it in abeyance long enough for insight to occur—he will learn the most wonderful process through which knowledge overcomes fear as sunlight purifies diseased surfaces. Floating on water is not a technique or skill to be learned; rather, it is sensing the element so fully that there is instinctive cooperation with it; and whatever one knows well—not technically or intellectually, but with the full flavor of kinship—one never fears. If you have once felt the functioning of a faculty in yourself beyond and above reason, you will probably be willing to "put your weight on it," until little by little, it finally becomes the very headquarters of your existence.

At first, in small ways, you will feel a hunch and notice it becomes borne out in due course; but as the process grows, you may very well learn that the test of reason does not apply and that you may need to wait a long time to see the wisdom of certain promptings that came to you. To the beginner, it is a most difficult phase when he oscillates between self-trust and distrust—wanting so much to return to the good, "safe" handholds at the edge of the wharf and leave the swimming to somebody else! Reason, then, seems a very comfortable raft to cling to—however limited in its reach—and ignorance has a cozy sound. Sooner or later, however, the urge to venture forth outweighs every fear and impulse to retreat.

5. BLOSSOM AND BLIGHT: A QUESTION OF SELECTION AND CULTIVATION

PHENOMENAL things sometimes occur very early in the process, and it is best to look at them and get them out of the way, for they are relatively unimportant. Some examples may be given.

You develop the largely reliable capacity to sense the contents of today's mail before it ever arrives. You know of the approach of a visitor, though you have not been told. You are lost and boy scout training plus reason tells you to go *that* way, but your feet seem fairly to be turning in their shoes, and so you let them have their way. They were right, as it turns out. "This is not the day to go to town," you think—unreasonably. It turns out to be a day of mishaps and Johnny comes down with a cold; yet all was quiet to start with. You make a daring decision of some kind wholly prompted by a sense of "rightness" which is inexplicable; you find that it bears fruit. You expect to be awakened at a given time in the night or early morning, and invariably, you are. You are startled at a sound slightly in advance of the cause which produced it; you see a sight shortly before it is apparent to the physical eyes. You are aware of the thoughts of people at a distance which are directed toward you.

However amazing and amusing these experiences seem, they are not important unless they lead into the deeper recesses of intuition. We may enjoy the convenience of lower forms of psychic perception when they become fairly reliable, but they do not make us better or more useful people, and they do not make us happier.

No sincere and truly intelligent person is going to let himself be content with a few psychic talents. His friends, if he tells them of these experiences, will no doubt feel that he is quite a clever fellow; and the chances are, the more clever he feels himself to be, the more short-lived will be his talents. It cannot be said too often that in back of all phenomena is a philosophical, highly moral set of contingencies. It is a moral universe in the sense that the highest wisdom flourishes only in the framework of established laws, and these laws are for the common good and are based upon perfect justice. How do we know? Well, a careful acquaintance with effects leads to an understanding of causes. Examine any plant carefully enough, and you are bound to discover some of the facts pertaining to the soil in which it was grown. There is also a "broad gate" to destruction, and it is just as easy to find as the Bible suggests. If there is justice in free will—and no one would deny it—then there must be an alternative to good. That one may become proficient in evil by observation and deliberate misuse of law is perfectly true. The gambler who exploits his patrons does so by perfectly understanding the way in which his mechanical roulette wheel is supposed to work, according to chance, and then by deliberately tampering with these laws. He will perhaps grow rich. It is questionable whether he will grow happy, and it is rather apparent that he endangers the welfare of others.

Before creating the impression that one must be a good, virtuous Sunday school goer in order to become intuitive, it may be suggested that "morality" is a much abused word. There is a petty, kindergarten morality to which we resort when we are too lazy or incompetent to discriminate, and to which we adhere chiefly in a desire to be both safe and right. Morality, in its highest sense, is the greatest good to the *whole*, and the consideration of that kind of morality may very well call for action which is quite beyond the pale, socially or from the standpoint of unimaginative ethics. However, let anyone rationalize this principle, and see where he lands!

We hold with Polonius that the greatest moral obligation is to oneself. "This above all, to thine own self be true, and it follows as the night the day, thou canst not then be false to any man." Here, without doubt, is one of the most important equations ever given to man. The absence of falsity must surely direct us toward greater usefulness. To lacquer on virtue according to established mores and customs is surely the very epitome of falseness. To do what is moral in the highest sense, we must therefore often offend the petty morality consciousness. To have a clear and uncolored understanding of the best individual intent, one must see intuitively; but to see intuitively, one must first take an uncompromisingly honest look at one's own motives. Hereby hangs probably the most important aspect of the discussion.

It is a very sad fact that once one gets a few reliable intuitive impressions, there is a real tendency to feel as though one has suddenly become a bit precious. The selfish, personal ego insists upon bringing even the most valid experiences of insight down into the mire of vanity and self-righteousness. Not one of us is a total exception, simply because absence from these ugly traits seems to come only after the most grueling process of self-inspection and reorientation. The loftier our moments of realization, the greater is the pull from below, so that what were rather mild affectations suddenly grow into serious vices. If we were inclined to be a bit prideful and opinionated before, we suddenly discover ourselves making the grossest blunders due to these hidden faults having sprung into full and poisonous blossom.

Perhaps the best place to start is to acknowledge at the outset that all of us are living under many illusions regarding ourselves, and that we need to be braced for the first rude shock that this is so. This is no easy encounter. There is absolutely no pain quite so excruciating as the discovery of one's own shallowness, hypocrisy and selfishness of motive. These are mass traits, carefully camouflaged under a coat of social veneer. If we expect to find them in ourselves, we will be that much ahead to start with. Even so, the ordeal of hide-and-seek—the mind struggling to cover up the mess, and the intuition bent upon revealing it—will result in an ever more complex system of self-delusion which daily becomes compounded until the individual gets himself into such difficult straits that he *has* to take a clearer look at himself. Nature crowds him from all sides, and he must suffer or yield up his petty conceit. It is very easy to think one is acting by intuition when all the time it is a very insidious imitator—the voice of one's own selfish desires. It has been said that intuition impersonally acts for the good of the whole. If it is the real thing, it cannot advise one person at the expense of others.

This does not mean that intuitive action will always lead to the immediate happiness of one's associates. It would be a fatuous kind of intelligence that operated with such limited meaning. The intuitionist is sometimes forced to act in a way that brings real pain to others. But if this force is the omniscient wisdom it is claimed to be, then it is bent upon freeing all whom it touches from the thralldom of self-deceit. It sees this intention as the greatest good, and obviously it is so, for out of self-deceit is born error, and error creates misery. The hotbed of self-deceit is desire. Action which grows out of personal desire is not perspective. As long as we have an idea in our heads about what would be nice to have happen to us—what we think we ought to do or cannot possibly do; as long, in other words, as we try to keep strings on our intuition—to make it tell us what we *want* to hear, then we are headed for the rocks.

Intuition will not necessarily give a person the answer to his dreams at all; it may rough him up and kick him around quite a lot—leading him here and there and turning him inside out so that every hidden surface of his nature is exposed to the light. But ultimately, if he endures the process, he will see the logic of all of it. He will suddenly find maturity and a sense of time and place. And whatever he had thought he wanted, he now finds all of that has changed, and he thanks the eternal laws that it is so; for now all the debris is cleared away and he sees his work and experiences the real and lasting symptoms of a growing peace and an increased usefulness. All of this can happen in such a relatively short time that one is quite literally, through forced insight, reborn into a new life where the poses and pursuits of a few years ago seem like the antics of a child.

To return to phenomena—it is not uncommon for people to have hunches which prove to be accurate. Women seem particularly adept at this kind of experience, which accounts for the widespread belief in woman's intuition. For example, the neighbor lady glowingly recounts her shopping experience—how she was after just such and such a dress for the bridge luncheon. She had a hunch to go down to a particular shop, and there it was. This is hardly an intuitive person, though she may claim to be. Desire can lead to direct results, if the desire is held firmly enough and long enough; but the results of personal and selfish desire delay evolution. It might be pointed out that the neighbor got her dress, and since it was a fairly harmless desire, why not?

Perhaps it is all right for the many individuals who must follow the impulse of their desires continuously and most of their lives, ending up on their deathbeds as trivial, childish people. But some, according to their development, may find that desire leads them into foolish and harmful circumstances, and they may wish to be rid of the selfish flavor in all of their affairs. One woman spoke ruefully of having practiced the metaphysical exercise of trying to materialize her desire for a new automobile. She got the automobile all right, but shortly afterwards, there was a terrible accident. She was more sensitive than the neighbor lady, and the experience jarred her into intuitive awareness of her own shortsightedness. Suppose the neighbor lady were a little more aware. She might have an "awakening" experience of her own. After all the fuss and bother, perhaps she spills a cup of hot coffee down her dress front, scalding herself and ruining the dress. In a flash, she sees the waste and stupidity of all the energy that has gone into so trivial an occupation as hunting for just the right dress. She may even begin to wonder what she is doing sitting there playing bridge while Rome burns!

The fact is that desire is creative, and we are all shaping our lives according to our desires. The more well-grooved we become, the harder it is to break up the pattern, for habit creates an unconscious desire to continue in familiar paths. If desire is coupled with ignorance, the results are bound to be bad—a principle which accounts for the state of the world today. Not all people, however, are capable of a strongly dynamic thought. Nor are all the desires of the dynamic ones held with dynamic intensity. So certainly, all desires do not prove out specifically; nevertheless, they will have a shaping effect upon the whole picture, and the more obsessed one becomes with a given desire, the more certain he is to fulfill it. If it is a pure and unselfish desire—an intuitive volition—so much the better. But such are rare as virtue itself.

Growth is transformation from one set of conditions to another which is higher or better. In the process, something has to give. The things that have to give way as we grow spiritually or intuitionally are the selfish things. So it is rather foolish to suppose that we can go out with a trivial motive and call our gambler's luck intuition. Nor, on the other hand, can we suddenly throw away everything in a desire for virtue and intuition. Desire, however directed, is an attempt to draw future conditions into the framework of today's insight. But both subject and object are bound to change. *Growth is transformation;* it is the voluntary yielding up of something that we realize with conviction is inferior and unworthy of us. This realization has to be complete so that the struggle ceases. If a man who has been cheating himself at solitaire for years suddenly realizes that there is no point to the game, he does not have to struggle with himself; he would no doubt just quietly get up from his chair, put the cards away and never be in the least tempted to return to the experience. Our self-deceptions are multitudinous and far more subtle than cheating at solitaire, but the principle is the same. As someone said of one of the more obvious destructive practices—that of drinking—"I don't just want to stop drinking; I want to stop *wanting* to drink!" We stop wanting our various physical and psychological crutches when we fully realize their worthlessness—not just intellectually, but intuitively, which is to feel through one's whole being with a total conviction. We may not even know what the "something better" is to replace that which we are convinced we no longer want, but we have at least cleared the way for it to come into being.

6. SYNTHESIZING THE PROCESS

INTUITION is always and invariably right, but until one becomes practiced in the attitude of "listening," many voices may be mistaken for intuition. Habit, training, desire and the activity of a certain mischievous element in invisible nature may very well color intuition and render it valueless. How are we to know, then, and isn't it dangerous to try to find out? There is no question about it, it *is* dangerous. And here is where judgment and discrimination enter the picture. If "intuition" suggests an action which is totally outlandish and contrary to one's notion of intelligent action, it is best to beware of it. Intuition tends to unfold in gentle sequence, though the rapidity of certain phases of unfoldment may very well make it seem ruthless. However, there is a sequence in this unfoldment, and the ground does not give way under established habits until one is psychologically prepared to take the next step. Always, in the background of one's experience, there is a silently growing rationale to substantiate the day-to-day metamorphosis. It means that the aspirant must look deeply into himself for this rationale, and sense out the links in the scheme that prompts his actions. This is the real key to whether or not action is intuitive. Then, every split second of the time, he must search out his motives and remorselessly cast out the unworthy ones—the limited, petty, selfish ones. This does not mean that he is to experience no enjoyment, but that he trusts his intuition to discover these enjoyments. People generally feel it is good to seek recreation; it is wholly unnecessary if one lives intuitively, for recreation will be there without asking, and all that could be wished for of healthy enjoyment comes as a natural accompaniment to the fact of living intuitively. Enjoyment; not indulgence. Again, morality is expedient. We obey traffic rules because we very well know that if we do not, we shall kill ourselves and some other people. At the same time, it is an impressive sight to watch the movement in a great traffic circle and to notice the preeminent spirit of cooperation that is intrinsic in this fact of "following the rules." It is one time when there is mutual agreement, quite impersonally, and the possibilities of brotherhood are dimly felt.

It may be felt that this action of the intuition seems autocratic and, in our democratic age, one hesitates at anything that smacks of authoritarianism. Nature, however, *is* authoritarian! Can we do anything, however much we try, to stop recurring rains, floods, earthquakes, volcanic eruptions and the rest? Nature in man is the only kind of authority a self-respecting individual wishes to submit to, but it requires intelligence and initiative to understand and cooperate with the laws of nature. We may assist into being certain floral and animal forms that were not there to begin with, but we must always work through nature's laws, which are unswerving. We are the products of nature—our minds, bodies and functions all came into being through the dictates of nature. Then why should we be shocked at the suggestion that the ethical and moral aspects of life also have their modus operandi in the invisible realms of nature? If this is so, then growth is not so much a matter of taking an original "shape" as it is of discovering what that shape was intended to be. It can be discovered, because it is already there intrinsically; only the right of free choice has led us away from it. A tree may be deflected by the pressures about it to grow in a crooked shape. This doesn't mean that it was intended to grow in that way. The tree did not choose. Circumstances shaped it.

We can and do choose the shape we shall take, and no one can observe human nature closely without sensing the heart-breaking disparity that exists between the expressed and the implied selves. So if it horrifies the intellectuals that we advocate a discovery of the moral and ethical rules that govern the universe, that are intrinsic in nature and in each one of us, then we can only say that they are the "unrealistic" ones (how often is an intuitive person accused of being "unrealistic"!) for failing to take into account the inevitable. If you are told that it is raining outside and you cannot see the rain, it does not change the fact. Yet knowledge of the fact obviously lends orderliness to your day.

If there is anything this world needs more than all else, it is to study nature intensively—her forms, her seasons, her ways—both in the woods and in our own bodies and minds. It has been said so many times and seldom heeded that all we need to know is exemplified in nature, if we would just become quiet and observant enough to see it. Watching and learning from nature has come to be an occupation associated with the nursery, with Rousseau, poets, artists and other "visionaries," and to have no practical meaning in our civilized, sophisticated world. Surely nothing is more practical than learning the intended meaning and function of our own beings. We cannot even begin to live significantly until that happens.

If we once catch the full truth of what has just been stated —that we cannot begin to live until we understand ourselves in relationship to nature—then a great change takes place. It must take place. Whatever we think our commitments are to our friends, family and society, at the moment that intuitive insight comes, we have no obligation more important than to pursue its meaning in our own, individual way—whatever it is. It is no good to say "I will wait until I've fulfilled all my obligations. I'll save up my money and then I will take time off to get quiet and see this thing through." It will never happen that way. Life continues to crowd, and we everlastingly continue to think that something is more important or needs tending to. This belief is helped along by all the good people who think they know what a man's duty is!

If the premise is true that by following the intuitive path, one may in time come to be infinitely more useful to himself and mankind, then where does his obligation lie? We are back to Polonius' equation. It isn't just good advice or sound reasoning, it's a maxim—a fact in nature. The test is whether a person can stand the abuse of the well-meaning friends and have the maturity and discrimination to see his first obligation, whatever kind of a ne'er-do-well it causes him to seem in the eyes of society. The people who count will respect his integrity; the rest will fall away, which is as it should be.

There is only one thing to say about the possibility of making mistakes. You will make them. Anyone would, and the more intent you are upon being perfect and missing no turns, the more cramped you will get until the strain becomes unbearable. In trying to be perfect, we are going absolutely contrary to the intention of the intuitive process, which is to show us our weaknesses and turn us into strong, dynamic individuals with a worthy purpose in life. The man who tries to force the process—to be always immaculate—will have to face at last the fact that his very effort is born of pride, which is one of the most common and ruinous weaknesses of all. There is that in each man which is very nearly perfect—that self, soul or principle from whence intuition springs. But those of us who are concerned with this book are not so perfected in our intuitional observation that we can look upon ourselves as anything but very erring and imperfect beings.

There is a way to look at this fact without losing one's balance. Let the mind be content that there is something wholly worthy in each person, albeit undiscovered. Then the attention is turned to the machinery of the self as one would examine the imperfections of an automobile. There are those, of course, who are so prideful of their possessions that they will even fail to admit the defects in their automobiles, so close is the identification between "me" and "mine." But most of us accept that even the best cars have imperfections, and we—if we are mechanically inclined—keep an ear tuned regularly to any indication of failure in proper function. In the same way, the intuitionist must keep his ear tuned to himself, accepting his vulnerabilities and defects, intent upon only one thing—ferreting them out and dealing with them directly.

The analogy is intended to take the element of conscience out of the observation, and give it a completely impersonal atmosphere. If one is bent upon self-discovery—seriously and honestly—this is in itself the highest morality factor to which he could possibly aspire. We might say that it undercuts all of his other weaknesses, so that is enough virtue to stand on, for the time being. Conscience has meaning only at lower levels of awareness, just as fear does. The intuitionist completely outgrows fear, as well as conscience in its limited sense. His activating principles are too broad and inclusive to be put to the waste and inconvenience of painful self-recrimination at every evidence of error, for these evidences are very numerous during the process of unfoldment, and if he must feel pain over each one, he will wear out and die of some nervous disease before he has got himself clear of the brush. He must be very mature, very objective, judging himself neither too leniently nor too strictly, and withal judging himself as impersonally as he would his automobile.

There is another aspect of this business of making mistakes. The very word has a foolish, moral overtone that makes one remember the way one felt back in grade school. In one sense, there is no such thing as a mistake. We are all struggling consciously or unconsciously to find out what life is all about. It may be very necessary for us to do foolish things over and over again until their power of attraction has ceased. If we must, we must. Trial and error is a long, hard method, conducive to much waste and destruction; but for most of us, it is the only way. Even the more intelligent ones are likely to need to repeat and repeat. But as intuition comes to supplant intellect, the trial and error method will tend to yield to direct insight.

On the other hand, we may, as do countless numbers of people, simply obey the dictates of the majority. It makes us feel safe to think the same things as everyone else, and to have our friends and neighbors looking at the world pretty much in the same way that we do. Blessed is the man who will follow his urges—even though they be reckless ones—repeating his mistakes and painfully finding his way to understanding, by comparison with the walled-up ones! Conservative people will sit by and chide him for his mistakes. But is anything a mistake which springs from a burning desire to find out the truth —actually and personally, not just through hearsay? Probably most people who are deeply intuitive begin their unfoldment in just this hectic way.

7. FUNCTION AND FLORESCENCE

WHAT OF the practical issues of life and the feeling common to everyone that they like to see something tangible for their efforts; is it possible to live the intuitive life and still find a harmonious relationship to the world of activities? Perhaps this is the question raised most frequently by all who contemplate these matters. The complaint is phrased something like this: "It's all well and good for you dreamers and visionaries to contemplate such lofty sentiments, but me—I'm a practical person. The world would fall apart if some of us did not think along practical lines." The fallacy of such a notion has already been suggested, but it may well be enlarged upon.

In the first place, no such horde of people is going to rush away from factories and fields and devote itself to the job of self-understanding, so we can pass over the threat. A few people may be inspired by insight, and their lives may very well fall apart. Indeed they must, because the sham structure must be razed before the permanent one can take its place —permanent in the sense of its being built upon solid and eternal principles which are so wonderfully complex that they contain an application for each step of the way. The busy ones—the ones who have no time for intuitive contemplation—are busy, many of them, doing superficial things. Why do we assume that our civilized inventions and conventions are wise and good just because they are clever? There is such an enormous difference between being clever and being farsighted!

Surely if one is to be truly practical, it is important to find out what is worth doing. This is the intensive search which occupies the early years of intuitive unfoldment. There does come a time when one begins to see interiorly the actual and unadulterated view of things, somewhat after the fashion of an aerial map. From this position, it becomes clear where the real need lies—what social tendencies need to be encouraged and which ones discouraged—for one sees to some extent through the eye of nature herself. At this point, there is the crying urge, almost stronger than life itself, to jump in and do something; but any such effort is promptly squelched. Finally, there is an awareness of a common "bloodstream" that pulses through us all, and it is observed that each of us individually has his peculiar shape, function and season. To act outside the rhythmic flow of spontaneous production is to distort the intended shape of the Whole. At last what one is to do becomes clear through signs that are unmistakable. Then there is the glad feeling of teamwork, the certain knowledge that if one gives his best in the directions indicated, he will not have lived in vain. Yet, in his eagerness, he will be impulsive. He will perhaps suddenly revert to intellectual methods; but inexorably, the pressures will show him not only the direction, but also the method that must be used. He has only to listen attentively, to watch very carefully, to keep close to his own center.

In this last thought is contained the keynote to all of his activities henceforth. Once he begins to try to accomplish, he will feel the weight of an enormous conglomerate of opposition against him. His discarded habits will wish to return; his well-meaning friends (if he has any left by now!) will be full of advice and various forms of psychological coercion. In a word, the vast majority will be opposed to him and his views and methods.

There is a very good reason why this is so. The impetus of thousands of people working contrary to the laws of nature has given to the mass mind a particular shape—distorted and unnatural, but strong by virtue of quantity. Anyone who "returns to nature" pulls against that unnatural shape, which creates reaction. Sooner or later, the intuitionist learns to treat this condition with respect and wariness, for it will otherwise be the ruin of him.

Nor at any time is he permitted to indulge an uncharitable notion toward those who oppose him, for—however mistaken and destructive—we are all equally dear to the heart of nature, if such a phrase may be used without too sentimental an interpretation. Nature is impersonal, yet no one's need is overlooked in her scheme; each is valuable and necessary to the Whole. So, the intuitionist must perpetually struggle to maintain his vision, his quiet rationale, in the face of every show of opposition; and he must be perpetually yielding up his own limitations in favor of an ever-broadening consciousness. It is not easy; it is perhaps the most difficult task known to man to maintain equilibrium in the face of all of this, yet there is a way to "ride the breakers" in comparative safety. The answer lies in the suggestion that he must keep close to his own center.

In every problem that arises or can arise—in every emergency of life—the first place to look is to oneself. In equilibrium, all things are solved. When the road being followed seems to drop off into space, we tend to get frantic as ants do when they lose the scent. We race around in circles and exhaust ourselves with effort of various kinds, all the time suffering feelings of insecurity and fear. There are seldom any emergencies so great that there is not time to grow quiet, to pull to the center. And even when instantaneous action is called for, it is usually instinctive and right. It is when we have time to reason and insist upon doing so that we muddle things. The answer is sitting quietly there in the supposed chaos, but it takes a quiet mind to sense its presence. It is reminiscent of those picture puzzles we used to stare at as children—a landscape in which is concealed a portrait of Abraham Lincoln or some other personage. Without reasoning our way from one figure to another—which we find only confounds us—we instead focus upon the whole, and suddenly the portrait emerges clearly.

In intuitive living, events are shaped from within outward. Keeping close to the center is like the process of the gardener, who nourishes the seed of his plant with proper soil, sun and water. The seed is everything; it is the cause behind all effects to materialize. The less one becomes distracted with the external effects, the better he can concentrate on his own center.

To say it in another way: it is not necessary to plan the events of life, beyond the most obvious ones such as packing for a trip or planning a shopping list. It is as though there is an invisible system of rays that reach out from the center of each of us and sets in motion the necessary forces to shape the material environment. This shaping action depends only (a very important "only" it is, however) upon the dynamic process going on at the center of one's own being during the struggle for intuition. The very struggle is an effort to bring an end to effort, the struggle to cease struggling. Our reason, our habits and training all suggest to us that we must struggle, we must reason, we must be perpetually doing something, or how shall we be useful? Eventually, we see the error in all of that, and we become quiet and tend our fires at the center. Then the sparks that are given off flow out and become a veritable system of worlds that shapes a universe in which the individual is the creator. This is what nature had in mind for us all along.

Perhaps there is a feeling that individual initiative has been lost somewhere along the line with all this talk about automatic action and the process of selection that goes on apart from choice. So far as we can see, there is no time in a man's development when he is not free to shape his own destiny. Certain causes are at work in our society over which he has no control and which to some extent will have their effect upon him, but the way in which he reacts to the various pressures and influences about him is the determining factor in his own freedom and sense of well-being. Also, the way in which he is reacting today will determine his future status.

for we continually attract to ourselves those conditions which depict our needs, limitations and desires. There is a super-conscious level—the area of intuitive insight—at which the status of the individual and his various correlations are perceived at a glance. This statement needs clarification.

At no time are we permitted to know the complete details of our future, and the most skilled prophet would have a hard time predicting in the face of the just law that decrees that we may experience hints and flashes, but never does the whole piece make itself visible in detail. It does not take a great deal of intelligence to see the wisdom of this, since evolution is clearly a question of individual initiative. However, the sensitivities of the intuitionist are attuned to what we might call the "theme" of his endeavor. He feels certain predominant motifs very strongly. We might say that he senses in himself the causes of future effects, causes which were with him at birth—shaped by his particular talents, hereditary influences, the environment into which he "dropped," and other more subtle factors.

Any writer or composer is familiar with a nice, mathematical principle that operates unvaryingly in the process of composition. He finds that under the strong influence of his theme, his composition shapes itself into a pattern in which every part is in some way an offshoot or a correlative of the main statement. He has only to conceive this theme perfectly in order to witness the almost automatic follow-through, as one who has pushed a boulder over the side of a cliff may expect and observe certain inevitable effects—the flowing cascade of pebbles that descend in the wake of the first action. Most artists will agree that creation is very little a reasoning process; that rather, having set certain concepts into motion, one may almost take the position of an alert and cooperative onlooker, who watches the effects he has produced.

It is the cognizance of this interesting process that permits one to sense the possibilities for intuitive living. One may feel the theme of his own life so strongly that he need not understand the details of his future in order to live creatively. He simply knows that where a theme is strongly felt, the resultant correlations are inevitable. If he insists upon a planning with his mind for future effects that he can count on, he will surely be disappointed and will miss altogether the great soul-satisfying leaps that are possible in intuitive living.

8. FIRST FRUITS

THE WORD "asceticism" is one of those charged words that can hardly stand alone, but must arouse in the one who uses it a strong feeling of antipathy or attraction, and often a frustrating mixture of both. Our dictionary gives the following definition: "The belief that one can attain to a high intellectual or spiritual level through solitude, mortification of the flesh, and devotional contemplation." The definition manages to connote a state of felicity irrationally mixed with the idea of painful self-restraint and even self-punishment. No wonder we are confused! Yet we find the word popping up continually whenever and wherever there is talk of spiritual development. Since it is to be used, it must be understood and qualified to suit individual situations and frames of reference. To one man, a person who does not smoke or drink may be thought ascetic, while to another, the line would have to be drawn much finer.

There are innumerable practices fashionable among those who aspire to the life of the spirit which range from physical posturing to confined diets of various sorts. While some of them have value in proper context, often the one-pointedness with which one's particular enthusiasm is pursued—without reference to a larger framework of principles—robs it of its efficacy and brings a condition of lopsidedness.

The more cautious advocates of asceticism will recommend a happy medium, but who is to say what this is? Can anyone prescribe a way of life that is a happy medium? Not without bucking against the problem of relativity, which has a decided modifying effect when it comes to the question of finding out what is true. Is there a way to approach the question, then, in order to discover a principle from which to work? It has been suggested already that every problem has a formula which is not an answer in itself, but which has in its dynamic ingredients the very essence of right application.

To indulge oneself and to acquire things is one kind of very pleasurable experience; to give up things—to sacrifice and deny oneself—is another kind of pleasurable experience, and there is neither merit nor demerit in either, nor does either lead to freedom. How we long for a prescription, a set of practices which says "do this" and "avoid that," for then we would not have to feel out the texture of things ourselves and learn what is true for you or me and for today only! For truth is not discovered in the flat surface of life, but in its movement and dimension. Although human bodies have certain mechanical similarities, the thousand-and-one subtle differences between the organic needs of one individual alone and those of another—to say nothing of the temperamental differences—make absurd any effort to prescribe a way of life for all. A diet which is perfectly suitable for one would make another miserable; and so it goes with exercise, environment, medicine and the rest.

Nevertheless, there are qualifying circumstances to suit the aspiring intuitionist as there are in other phases of life. An athlete knows that he cannot go without sleep, eat rich, fattening food, smoke heavily and still maintain and increase his skill in the field of sports. A violinist knows that he cannot work as a plumber or carpenter by day and be ready for the concert stage in the evening. In these instances, the capacities and limitations of the human body are readily grasped, and because the athlete and the violinist presumably prefer their chosen professions, they think little of the sacrifices made in order to pursue them. The "sting" of sacrifice is not present, for common sense assures them of *no other course of action being possible to them under the circumstances.* When we know beyond the shadow of a doubt what is right for us to do, we do not mind doing it. The frustration of choice and discipline do not enter.

Assuming that one has a faint glimpse of the possibilities for freedom and usefulness through living the intuitive life, then it soon becomes apparent that this life is dependent upon the discovery and development of the necessary faculties, which are not developed alike in everyone. And just as the athlete is developing skill and precision through a recognition of the nature of his body, so the person who yearns for increased sensitivity of an intuitive nature will come to recognize that these faculties require something of the status of the athlete, whose abstemiousness is part of this training.

The intuitive process itself suggests to the growing "sensitive" the course to be taken. He does not reason out what his practices shall be; he simply lives with his senses open to direction, and in a most profound way—if he is earnest and not just toying with a new idea—the way of his life will be indicated from hour to hour. In the beginning, he may simply see the truth—that a general house-cleaning is in order—that he must get himself uncluttered and free of dependency upon the luxurious living that is common to our century. In his eagerness, he may go to extremes, but in time, his senses will report to him without prejudice. But whatever alteration in practice he accepts, it must come with the same sense of certainty that makes the athlete know what he must do to increase his skill, *and there must be the same absence of regret through knowing that what is coming to replace that which is given up, is infinitely more to be desired than was the former.*

An ascetic is commonly thought of as one who gives up things that he would prefer to keep. But one who is wisely abstemious—not from reasoning or reading or self-righteousness—has only given up things which no longer matter to him, and thus he cannot be said to be making any sacrifices. If we say, rather, that an exchange is taking place, we will be closer to the truth in all of its subtle ramifications. This renewal may be consciously governed by the individual in such a way as to change his affinities completely—his way of life, his thought, his morals, his sensitivity and receptivity. However, the aspirant learns what the statement means for himself.

His attitude toward dependency has a decided shaping effect upon the intuitionist's way of life. There is no object in any type of philosophy which does not make for personal freedom. The more dependent we are upon things, people, ideas, the more ensnared we are. Perhaps the theme of our materialistic world's strivings might be stated thus: "I want to be rich enough and influential enough to do what I please; then I'll be free." The fact is, however, that money conditions our choices and therefore hinders the intuitive process. Yet our unimaginative minds can conceive of no type of freedom that is not bought. Some of us talk a great deal about psychological freedom through an "integrated personality," but any individual who shapes himself comfortably to the status quo—who so vacillates and compromises and placates as neither to give nor take offense in a world which must offend his highest sensibilities—is not happy; he is only mesmerized. If he keeps adjusting himself to everything he meets so as to feel safe, he may live thus to the end of his days in relative comfort. For most people that is enough, and they do not mind that the world is riven with mold and worm holes under the shining surface of things they hold dear. They will not see that their indifference is breeding future chaos for the generations to come. And they are deeply, insufferably dependent.

If one is really intent upon the discovery of truth, then an excellent place to start is by examining the various props and accoutrements of our civilized society. We are so accustomed to the paraphernalia of our environment that it is almost impossible to imagine life without it. We are not suggesting that one should either have things or not have them; but rather that it is important to be free and objective enough to decide what one really does want, instead of being a slave to custom. And how can this freedom of choice come about unless there is experiment and searching enquiry? The tragedy of modern living is that there is really no freedom of choice. Social and commercial influences are so great that they shape the individual's life regardless of his inmost preferences. But suppose one were to see this, and were willing to try pleasing himself instead of public opinion; there is no doubt that his habits would change.

Notice the joy and sense of release apparent among a group of campers on a holiday, who have temporarily reduced their living requirements to simplicity. How very different is the easygoing, tolerant spirit that prevails—the permissive atmosphere that surrounds the children, the carefree return to youth that comes to the adults! And notice the dull, dead heaviness and sorrow that comes when they must "return to the grind." Yet we go on elaborating our living year in and year out under the illusion of timesaving devices and utility living.

If a person craves freedom above all other things in life, he will experiment deeply and unstintingly. He will take no "authority's" word for it in the matter of his physical and psychological requirements, but will strike off at a tangent from the main stream of traffic and explore his own deepest longings and urges—irrespective of what other people think. He will look at his own anatomy afresh and forget all about his conditioning. If he does this, he will discover some amazing facts about the amount and kind of food one must eat to sustain life and health. He will look at the matter of sleep afresh and question the "eight hours" theory. He will be suspicious of the gymnastic theories and the notions about heat and cold and vitamins and minerals. He will look deeply into the antisepsis notion—the basis of so much fear. If he really wants to know the truth as it pertains to himself from day to day, he will look and learn and be subtly, invisibly impressed from every direction. Then, when freedom of choice is gained, he will see how it yields to automatic action or intuition.

9. THE HARVEST: MATURATION AND CONTRIBUTION

SPIRITUAL insight is a result of self-discovery, and so all teachers and books place emphasis upon the factor of solitariness—to such an extent, in fact, that we lose sight of the truth that self-discovery can only become complete when it merges into integrated living. Insight that does not reveal the wholeness of life and the subtle relatedness that exists among all of us is not true insight. Intuition is not a subject confined to yogis and hermits. How can such an all-encompassing function of nature be a fact only in such and such a context? Intuition is operative in a great many people at odd moments, and our concern here is with a deliberate cultivation of the faculty. We cannot strain after it or force it into being, but we can cultivate it—that is, we can examine the environment of our sensitivities, and by pruning here and watering there, assist its growth.

Suppose we have come to the place where we see the necessity of a change in ourselves. We are weary of the incessant repetition of meaningless habits and pursuits, and we secretly determine to yield to those quiet promptings that come to us in the dead of night or in some isolated moment of acute perception inspired by the sight of a tree, a cloud, a waterfall. Instead of putting that moment regretfully aside, we encourage its meaning—as one blows on a tiny ember in order to bring a flame into being. We at last feel something substantial taking place inside of us. A new life is crying for expression and making us acutely and painfully conscious of the sad, pitiful waste that is the life of every one we know. Now comes the moment of decision. We address ourselves to this new life boldly. The action might be expressed in such words as these: "I know not your nature or where you will lead me, but my heart trusts you. Besides, nothing can be worse than to go on in this clumsy, blind dance of death that is my life. I am ready. Let nature have her way with me, for there is that in me of which nature is the servant—my God and my Guide. So let this new life happen . . . let it happen. . . ."

Such a decision will start the awesome machinery of the great laws into motion, so the aspirant needs to be certain that he means it. Henceforth, he must be choiceless and malleable as clay. There may be no hedging, no set of conditions in his agreement. He must yield up his life and all that it contains to the imponderable process which he has set in motion; but if he has actually arrived at the proper frame of mind for the great adventure, his fear of the unknown will be less than his eagerness *to know*. This state of mind and heart can and does come to a few people of all walks of life and in all nationalities and countries. Nature is omnipresent, so why should she confine her gifts to the holy man in a cave in the Orient, and leave the man who is burning out his heart in a New York office to his own miserable fate? All she requires is recognition, and at the moment any individual looks within himself and feels the promptings of what might be, at that moment he becomes a student of nature, in both its visible and invisible aspects.

The fateful decision means that the individual is prepared—come whatever—to be true to himself and his own highest understanding of what is right. With this decision, he immediately becomes a kind of catalyst in the midst of other people. As he ceases to pander to the hypocritical ways of society, his relationships quite naturally get redefined without any effort to do the job himself. *Just one person who acts with complete, unadulterated integrity can throw all into confusion about him; yet in that confusion, everyone has his opportunity to gain a fresh perspective for himself.* And suppose he loses his job and his friends . . . how does he know this is not the best thing after all? The intuitive life isn't for weaklings, but for courageous, honest people who understand that the old *must* give way if something new and worthier is to come into being. The fact remains that one cannot be true to oneself and harm others by that principle. Many and varied will be the circumstances that attend each individual situation, but in every case, there is a way and an answer. If the aspirant plays the game straight, nature will not let him down; and it is possible that neither will his mate. If the vision can become a mutual experience with both man and wife, then as a couple or a family, they may enter upon the intuitive life. *And here we have the beginnings of a new society, in which truth and cooperation are the very theme of existence.*

The environment may now undergo certain changes, so one needs to look at this matter of environment. Most of us cleave to an established environment because of fear. We may disregard this fear and plunge ahead, or we may—as most people do—entrench ourselves like people pursued by a perpetual enemy and build up an eternal arsenal for defense.

It is feeling safe that counts. With all the various precautionary measures to prevent accident and illness . . . with all the locks, bolts, bars and weapons that are employed by members of our society to give them solace, there is still no *feeling* of safety. One must be constantly on guard, forever fumbling with protective devices, and still there is fear. How can one always be sure that the key has been turned, that the loaded weapon will discharge properly, that an accident will not find one after all? And besides the numerous bodily threats, what of the love one cherishes, the job, the social position? The feeling of fear hurts; it is sheer pain—depleting, destructive of health and creative energy—yet most people live with it as does a cancer victim resigned to his disease. If we cannot remove the feeling of fear, there is no such thing as security. How can we think of the matter of environment apart from this feeling of fear?

Progress is generally thought of as the development of one's environment by means of talent and training in such a way that a tangible product is achieved—something useful to the world. In the proper time and place, this may be true; but we cannot precipitate that product prematurely. And in any case, results are not something static to be aimed at, but a gradual and accumulative outpouring from an abundant nature, which happens spontaneously and almost unconsciously.

For the rest of it, the intuitionist sees experience and environment as the means, not the end. The vital center of living is interior, and the environment becomes the laboratory from which we draw stimuli. Obviously, then, environment must be a flexible matter, and any attachment to environment is antagonistic to growth. Therefore, it is not pain, but satisfaction to step away from that which has served its purpose and into that which promises further stimuli to insight, or which is otherwise expedient and appropriate. It is very difficult to refrain from trying to precipitate results, for we have been raised in a society where the idea of security is the predominant drive.

There is a kind of security—a very questionable kind —which goes with walking out into the wilderness armed with guns, knives, traps and insulating materials. Then there is another kind which is arrived at by a much deeper and more arduous process, but nonetheless, results in real security. It comes about with understanding nature and entering into complete reconciliation with her. Then one is secure without arms. Everywhere, people are arming themselves—placing barriers against possible invasion from poverty, ridicule, disease and the rest. Actually, they are not so much protecting themselves as walling themselves in! If it is true (but even this is absurd) that they are making themselves safe from any harm, they are also largely making themselves safe from any lasting good. No matter how hard they try, they do not end up by feeling safe, and it is feeling safe that counts.

Wherever the person is when the insight hits, it becomes necessary to slow down and take a deep, searching look into the environment and way of life. At the same time, he will be examining the society in which he lives and moves, and which has such a powerful determining influence upon his affairs. If he is honest, he cannot help admitting the falseness of much that he sees. This is not want of love for society. To love humanity, we have to understand it—its weaknesses and strengths, its vulnerabilities and capabilities. If it is apparent that our society is sick, then we must first insulate ourselves against contagion; only then can we see about helping the situation. So we need pay no attention to the ones who will cry "Isolationist!" It is one thing to insulate and another to isolate; and social isolation is not the same as psychological isolation, which is selfish and harmful. But it may be observed that the latter condition exists throughout the world, and nowhere more obviously than in our metropolitan areas.

In America particularly, we like intimacy. We tend to share our most personal business with any interested and sympathetic party who happens along. Observed from a psychic standpoint, this tendency has a diluting effect upon our individual strength, and hence upon society as a whole. We seek people for excitement and stimulation, but mostly for sympathy. There will never be a strong and healthy society until individuals can find strength through independence. Observe nature and notice the orderly progression of the heavens, as each star holds its position in relationship to another. Imagine the chaos if this were not so! There is power and dignity and the right notion of love in solitariness. All of this is lost in the hectic overlapping of self on self in our present-day society.

The individual who would bring about a change for the better in society will look first askance upon his own immediate environment and way of life. Since most people's way of life is determined by the kind of job held by the family wage earner, it is necessary to look here first of all. A man and wife who see the truth—that their lives must undergo a tremendous upheaval if they are to learn to live by nature's laws—will be willing that the man shall quit his position if it brings him no real satisfaction, or if he finds that he sacrifices his integrity daily for the sake of income. Upon this step will naturally follow other modifications of a severe sort, but there is a glad feeling of relief and quiet adventure in this fateful decision. Above all, let him not be tempted back into the groove through fear, because for every couple who is deeply in earnest, there is a way.

Work and love are synonymous. If one is not too cynical and hardened by the world, it is nice to watch the birds at their nest-building and rearing their young. There is no effort or reluctance . . . no wondering if the job will suit some overseer or please some public. The bird is intent upon doing the very best job he can, simply because he loves his work and it is the expression of his heart. Man will never rise above the world's influence by placating and kowtowing; only by masterfully emanating his "idea" so strongly that the doors must open to admit him can he hope to gain the world's ear without forsaking his own soul. If the world rejects his effort, it is only because the idea is not clearly understood by himself. It must be purely formed and forcefully executed.

But the world's reaction or sanction should be only a secondary consideration in any case. The intuitionist does not have to sell his wares. If they are good, then they—coupled with what he himself has become—present a force which it is impossible for the world to overlook. When a new world throws out its satellites in the very vigor of its own creative process, the heavens must be informed of it, for they are altered by it. No good work can long remain secret, for first it is felt invisibly, then at last the manifest creation itself must be viewed.

To one who loves truth above all else, that truth yearns to find expression in the materials of life . . . in its various activities and forms. First it becomes manifest in the individual himself: in his way with others, with his family and with himself; it is expressed in his home and in his personal attributes and pursuits. Gradually, he presents a face to the world which cannot be ignored, simply because it is wholly different from the average. Whoever knows him will be affected by him, and already his "work" has begun in just this simple act of being himself without compromise.

Then, as his concepts grow, he may want to find other expressions for them—in writing, music, art, or other crafts —in a project of some sort. He may want to return to a new version of his old job. He does not say "Will this be pleasing to others? Will it earn me a living?" All of this is irrelevant and out of place in his very private and personal unfoldment. He should work first of all to give happy, overflowing expression to all the things that are in his heart, because he just can't help himself. It pleases him to do so; he feels enriched by it. By all of the observable laws, if he truly refuses to compromise and demands and extracts the right to unfold in his own way, creating from the fullness of his own heart, then he will realize the answer to his growing needs and supply will come—not as an end, but as a by-product. Never should he demean his soul by any other course of action.

A man and woman who are proper mates can both individually and as a team follow upon this wondrous way. And their children can be folded into the protective wings of the great laws and grow up free of the soul-crippling influences of our society. Consider the implications! Social, political and economic reforms will never accomplish what is possible to a few people who have grasped the true meaning of the intuitive rationale that hovers back of their lives, waiting to be discovered.

10. WITHIN THE GARDEN WALLS

IF IT IS true that too much intimacy and loss of self-sufficiency and independence distort relationships in the world, it must also be true of the marriage relationship. There never was and never will be any harmony created through sameness. Yet possessiveness and dependency are an attempt to absorb and to nullify opposition. Only in individual strength and steadfastness can complementary tendencies operate to produce harmony.

For some reason, we all have a tendency to separate our attitudes about relationships in general from those pertaining to our wives, husbands and children. And when we think of reform, it is usually with respect to the outer fringe of life. The special agony of reform within the intimate center of one's life is put off as long as possible. Yet here is the core of the infection—the place where ugliness and hypocrisy are born first thing in the morning and often renewed again in the evening. And here—where we are truly off guard—where our thoughts as we dress, as we eat, as we move about the house are giving a faithful record of our own impediments, is the true laboratory of self-discovery.

We marry because we are unfulfilled; if it were otherwise, we would probably not marry, for the average marriage offers little beyond a sense of repletion. After that, it is a struggle for identity—each battling for his own place in the scheme of things and usually feeling that the mate is the greatest obstacle to that identity.

The difficulty is that we allow no room for metamorphosis in marriage. We have a fixed idea, derived from many subconscious sources, of what the ideal marriage should be. We are always feeling a lack when, invariably, we change, our husbands or wives change, our environment changes, and withal, there seems to be no progressive center of gravity that moves along with these changes. When a man and wife mature in each other's company, the marriage state alters radically with the progressive needs and insight of the two related individuals. In marriage, as in all of life, there must be room for infinite flexibility, for when there is coercion by way of established ideas, an unresolvable conflict results.

An intelligent person comes to have faith in the process of metamorphosis—to see that his puny knowledge cannot fix the facts in the presence of the overwhelming movement of nature. One must, very early in one's marriage, release all of the ingredients—husband or wife, children, home, position—to move, to change, to shape in accordance with individual and group evolution. This requires a great deal of selflessness—to see the intuitive process taking hold of one's nearest and dearest concerns and to move with it instead of blocking it with cleaving and clinging, with ambition and personal desire. One must be prepared, if need be, to evolve clear out of the marriage relationship, if needs grow strongly incompatible. But this state must come as a natural step, not as an escape; for any relationship which is prematurely resolved will surely return in one form or another to be faced at a future date. The only way to be sure is to let the forces at work decide the issue, assuming that one is a conscientiously impartial spectator of his own affairs and not selfishly involved in the result.

Those who have stumbled through the metamorphosis of

early marriage years, when emotions are thick and palpable from the intimate intermingling of feelings and needs, and have then passed on to the more mature phases, find no words to express the incomparable wonder of this latter experience. They are usually content to dwell peacefully in its quiet atmosphere without the world being any the wiser. Perhaps if these few quiet ones would speak, and the romantic, volatile ones would be still awhile instead of shouting at us from every placard, magazine cover and motion picture screen . . . then the world would come to know what it misses.

When two who are mature and evolving spontaneously set out together to explore the reaches of marital relationship, something comes into being which is not marriage at all, as it is commonly understood; nor is it the absence of a state of marriage. In it, there is separateness and individual strength, and at the same time, a beautiful at-oneness. There is polarity of a most dynamic and creative nature, in the presence of which the most romantic tales of all times seem fit only for the nursery stages of life. But if one tries to find this state—if there is an effort to assume the superficial aspects of it without knowing the actual state itself through painstaking and self-less inquiry, no slightest good is gained. It is necessary to start way back in the simple exchange of everyday encounters and to notice carefully the motives, the thoughts, the acts, and to see if these are collectively producing a sturdy and enduring growth, or if this growth is sick and false and must one day be pruned back to the stump to begin over again.

Children bring a new threat and a new challenge to the marriage relationship—largely because of the fear that is connected with parenthood and especially motherhood. In many of the animal species, we observe the frenzy of devotion to the offspring based upon fear and the terrible, instinctive urgency to protect the young at any cost. It is easy enough to understand that on the animal level, nature's intention is to protect the various species from annihilation in the face of the countless threats of forest and jungle. But those of us who have become mothers in the human kingdom know that this fierce preoccupation with the welfare of our little ones does not leave off with the animals, but finds birth in us, and if we are of particularly nervous disposition, may even make our lives extremely uncomfortable, as we tire under the strain of continued watchfulness. Civilization brings freedom from many of the primitive threats, but it replaces these with some which, because of their obscure nature, are more agonizing to the mother. These threats often arise within the mother herself—her unsureness at her job, the feeling that she is not well-informed in psychological matters, the frustration she feels at being unable to provide what she considers to be the right social or economic environment for her child, and so forth.

There is certainly no possibility of solving the problems of parenthood without understanding related problems, such as relationship in general, one's attitude toward economic and social position and all the other matters touched upon in these pages. It is only when we have an intuitive grasp on these that we can intelligently approach the business of parenthood. Assuming that this is the case, then some revealing facts become uncovered.

We see that the painful and pathetic anxiety of the animal mother becomes an instinctive memory in the human mother—all out of proportion to the existing threats. Most mothers who worry over the physical welfare of their children a great deal admit that they recognize there is no justification for such anxiety, but they will say "I just can't help myself." To the person who is seriously searching into the meaning of life and the facts of his own nature, evolution can be an astonishingly rapid process. For instance, if a mother can come close enough to her anxiety to see that it is the product of an outgrown instinct, she can pass on into a higher phase of relationship to her child. Here, intuition comes into play, and she discovers at odd moments—which tend to increase in number—a delightful and perfect accord which signals the child's needs from hour to hour, while suggesting the wider scope of his welfare in general. She finds that the more she detaches herself from him—the less she is identified and emotionally concerned—the greater is her intuitive "hookup" with him.

It is not likely that one becomes selfless by trying, but it happens when one sees the far more desirable state possible through giving up the very things one loves most. It is not too much to say that no intuitive relationship is possible for a mother until she has literally given over her child to the forces of nature, of which she herself becomes a mere instrument. It is the knowledge that these forces are all-prevailing and all-wise that makes an intuitive person. When she can yield her child to the persons and conditions which come naturally into the flow of his life, without desire to manipulate or interfere, then she is working with his destiny and not against it. It is a slow, painful process for a conscientious mother to learn to separate instinct from intuition and to let the latter prevail; but if there is real love, it is possible.

An intuitive parent recognizes above any other consideration, the obligation to life to rear a child who is in his turn susceptible to intuition. The fears about his physical welfare have become transcended, and in place of these is a deep and wholly impersonal sense of duty which sternly decrees that the parents perpetuate the principles of life to which they have fallen heir. Then it is that they understand something of the large framework of their job as parents. They begin to see humanity in their children and their children in humanity. They look searchingly into the state of the world, and to them are visible all the real threats that the insensitive parent notices not at all. They know, from their own struggles, that intuition is in the beginning a frail flame which is easily smothered in the frenzied atmosphere of commerce and competition, and in the static atmosphere of entertainment mediums. A child gorged with sights and sounds, tastes and smells arising from the main thoroughfare of life cannot see with his inner eye or hear with his inner ear; yet while he is young is the very time when his intuitive faculties are most likely to be struggling to express themselves. The parents will know that inasmuch as intuition is of nature, the environment of the child must include the things of nature, for these are the means of education.

Finally, intuitive parents discover that there is a marvelous correlation between the needs of each member of the family unit and that of the whole group; and that less is required of them than they may have supposed. All things needful to the child's growth and understanding are incipient in him, and given the right environment, the shape of the final product —the mature individual—will in all likelihood be somewhere near what it was intended to be. But right environment and right education must be discovered, for the prevailing systems do not allow for the intuitive way of life.

The intuitive family is not now secure by virtue of some sacred immunity. It experiences no divine protection against the calamities that befall other families, but it knows the special resiliency which attends the possession of principles to fit the major emergencies of life—even that of sudden death. Death is so fittingly and properly a function of nature that to abhor death is to mock the wisdom of nature.

The ways of nature in death are awesome indeed —unrelenting, to be sure, but the harsh moment is cushioned from many sides, as the close observer may learn. If we look very closely, we see that nature arranges the stage for death with careful artistry—like the great strategist she is—and only our nearsightedness makes us fail to see something grand and purposeful in her movements. But very few people are capable of observing death. The emotional response pattern of shock, grief and despair are so deeply ingrained in the culture, that there is no seeing . . . only feeling. And this feeling is the self-enclosed torture of a living death, compared with which nature's death—however violent—seems preferable.

But when one has learned to trust and cooperate with nature, then even death is something to be examined with attention and reverence. It is a prickly pear which the courageous may—with bleeding fingers—pluck open and find inside . . . the alkahest. So it is with the intuitionist. Nature whispers her clues to him well in advance of any crisis he may need to meet. These clues are like the words which form a verbless sentence. At the moment of crisis, the "verb" is supplied, and the mind records on the conscious level that for which it has been subconsciously preparing for many months, perhaps years. This is the intended function of premonition. But when we live carelessly—hourly violating nature's laws—no such benevolent process is experienced. When death strikes, we reach for the artificial anesthetic—the pill, the bit of brandy, the solace of tears and sentimental sympathy. Then we live on in the mental stasis of memory —the worst of all possible deaths.

11. SEEDLINGS: THE SCHOOL AS A LABORATORY OF NATURE

AMONG all of life's experiences, none is more resounding than the mysterious quickening that takes place when the mind of a natural teacher and the mind of an apt and eager pupil touch each other. This is a religious moment, and like all religious experiences, it is rare. No vast hedgework of learning institutions can ever capture it. On the contrary, systems of this sort more often discourage it.

However, given the two leading actors, this mysterious thing can happen almost anywhere—anywhere, that is, where nature is given a comfortable seat on the occasion. Because intelligence (not intellect) is of nature or God. The pleasantly sculped and sunlit plaza, the leisurely Greek bath, the quiet pagoda, the cool temple chamber, the small, unscheduled country school or, often, no more than a simple tutorial relationship under the shade of a tree, have been suitable sites in times past for the swift germination of knowledge. It is unlikely that they can be improved upon.

Poets, artists, and natural teachers are born with a pre-aged knowingness built into their ribs like the aged lumber in the hull of a ship. The learning situation is the teacher's natural element, capable of drawing out of him an ingrained talent, mysterious as are all talents. Confrontation with one or more expectant pupils is, for him, provocative of a peculiar inner transformation. Approaching the demands of the situation, he may be ailing, timid, ill-prepared, and trapped by the limited resources of a miserable, grumbling "self" totally unfit for the task. But let him once pass through the classroom door and he shakes out of this "self" as out of an ill-fitting shoe; and what is released expands and grows and there is authority in its voice and procedures.

I have experienced those charged moments in a classroom when the intent, upturned faces of a group of pupils were undifferentiated and lay in the path of knowledge like specks caught in a shred of light. My hackles would rise, and while I felt that in some difficult-to-describe fashion I was orchestrating the experience, it was not of me. It breathed out of the corners of the room and exuded from all objects and persons assembled like a sweat-born Presence.

For what is a teacher if not an instrument? The position of the teacher is critical in that one member of the group has to tend the fire and stir the brew out of which good mind-stuff arises. The teacher both acts and watches the action; is both involved and uninvolved. His or her job is to monitor events in the direction of THAT which is trying to happen. Communication is not just a two-way thing; it is a three-way thing. It is the teacher, the pupil, and THAT.

Instead of looking in the obvious places for the meaning of education—in the books, the universities, the lectures—let us try to look with greater simplicity and originality into the facts of human nature. When thought goes stale, it is because of the lateral sweep of men's ideas, which levels to conformity every tender, fertile prospect of new growth. But when anything truly fresh and vital works its way through the heart and mind of a stray genius, it always has that quality of deep penetration which comes from pressing at some specific point. Break up the individual unit, and you will know more of the mass of which it is a constituent; understand the underlying motive and prognostication of a single mind, and there may be found the ingredients of purposeful reconstruction.

When one observes human nature very closely, several kinds of motive force are discovered which prompt people's actions and shape their destinies, individually and then collectively. Educational systems are simply the outward expression of these types of motive force. Before a motive is forceful enough to condition the direction of one's life, there must be some kind of definition of values, either unconsciously felt or clearly intellectualized, as the case may be. So, it is important to observe and take note of the things that people consider valuable; then we will understand why we pursue certain ideas about education and life in general.

We are going to do what intellectuals call "over-simplifying." We will do this consciously, because a bone structure view gives a swift clarity that may be modified but not obliterated by further observation. If we note what it is that people want beneath their various activities and pursuits, we find that goals are surprisingly uniform. Most people want some comfort, both physical and psychological. At the same time, they want to occupy themselves with something that will be interesting while giving them a sense of significance.

The pursuit of comfort is expressed in the almost universal preoccupation with the material environment. In the same way that we fidget and readjust our bodies and props when settling down to a good book, we also endlessly manipulate the daily environment to serve our great lust for comfort. "Lust" is the word, for although we may express this powerful desire with moderation and restraint, still it insists itself through every other condition with a sustained and long-lived urgency. In many people it is the predominant motive force, so that the whole life is consciously or unconsciously dedicated to such occupations as will lead to periods of leisure which are as delicious as the mind and pocketbook will permit. Such people are governed by their external senses with respect to their basic orientation to life. They are easily recognizable in our society by the hunger with which they seek conveniences, luxury items, and pleasurable pastimes;

and by the enormous sacrifices they make in the interest of these pursuits.

For another type of individual, the mind constitutes the greatest realm of gratification. To such an individual, the material environment may be relatively unimportant. The accumulation of knowledge, the solving of intellectual enigmas, and, simply, the sustained exercise of the mental faculties upon everything which presents itself to the observation are the consuming concerns of the intellectual. He quite literally lives in his mind, and without the perpetual pursuits of the intellect, he feels lost and miserable.

For all practical purposes of study, nearly the whole of mankind may be parceled out over a range of states of mind and feeling which fall within the two extreme situations which have been pictured. The spiritual man—the man who has begun to crack the shell of his physical and mental environment—is comparatively rare. Because he is rare, his is certainly not the voice that shapes our policies and institutions as a human society. Yet, those who are prepared to concede that he exists—that there are some individuals who have assiduously cultivated in themselves an unobstructed observation of the meaning of life apart from and in combination with the physical senses—must also concede that his is the only perspective view; that he is the only individual prepared to provide any kind of definition of values suitable as a framework for human endeavor and for individual and collective good.

The intuitive individual, the seer, the person with range of vision and a grasp of universalities is epitomized in the names of certain revered philosophers whom we study superficially in philosophical survey courses at our universities, but whose teachings are rarely considered practical for our day. The prevailing educational systems represent the value commitments of people dominated by feeling and intellect. Education is purposefully directed toward two general goals: (1) to assist the child to find a comfortable place in society, if he is not especially gifted intellectually. By "comfortable" is meant that he will have sufficient means to insure as pleasing an environment as possible, and that he will so conduct himself as to find self-respect, usefulness, and acceptance among his associates; (2) to assist the gifted child to make as outstanding a contribution as possible in the artistic or intellectual "worlds," while maintaining his adjustability to the challenge of relationships in present-day society. It does *not* mean the deeper adjustment which comes with a perception of values which are unconditioned by time and social conditions. So it is important at the offset to decide whether we wish to approach the problem of education by means of existing value criteria and to perpetuate the prevailing goals, or if we wish to go deeper and find a soundly philosophical approach, whatever radical measures this may suggest.

Unfortunately, the history of educational philosophy gives us few men and women of real vision—those whom we might call "practical philosophers." Such individuals have little in common with the prevailing educational system; yet they hold value commitments in common, whether they lived two thousand years ago or live today.

It is important to differentiate between the "practical" philosopher and the academic or theoretical philosopher. The latter is usually a scholar and a collector of philosophical opinion and schools of thought. He may have achieved a degree of calm and insight and enjoy the respect of intellectuals, but he is unlikely to be what the Easterner would call "liberated" to any marked degree.

The practical philosopher may or may not be a scholar. In many cases, he would not be, because it is a strange fact that the kind of studiousness which turns a man into a scholar by Western standards has a way of interfering with the process of intuitive unfoldment. A practical philosopher is an individual who has devoted himself to such a highly sensitized observation of himself and the universe about him that he becomes aware of an orderly sequence of principles to be found in nature through direct experience. These principles give clues to the function and meaning of man in relationship to the universe, with implications for human conduct and aspiration.

The practical philosopher is a man of faculty. He knows that the external world has significance only in proportion to the cooperative, subjective awareness which he brings to his experience. Unlike the aspirations of most men, which he finds immature and without merit in his own realms of observation, his hopes and strivings have to do with the necessity he feels for aligning himself with the intent of nature. He is a humanitarian; not by choice or because he wishes to be virtuous, but because the trend of his accelerated evolution turns the surfaces of his being outward. The pleasure or pain which the average man receives from those things which pertain to the self and its immediate extensions—the family, the home, the car, the job and associates —these gradually alter until the practical philosopher has formed his identification with humanity as a whole, without in any way neglecting his immediate obligations. But these matters are inarticulate to the intellect alone. They suggest meaning only to the mind which has begun the process of intuition; and fortunately, there are those minds still to be found, even in our hapless civilization.

But what, now, is the difference between what the esotericist calls a liberated man (always a relative state, to be sure) and a mature or well-integrated man as measured by professional psychological criteria? We have devised ways to test the comparative adjustability of human beings; the degree to which one is able to live in a state of relative peace in relationship to the challenge of his environment and the inner struggles which this is likely to produce. Where there is an ability to accept a challenge with poise and equilibrium, to make choices with clarity, and to abide by these choices; and withal, to find an experience of joy and satisfaction in living, then we say that the individual is mature and has mental and emotional health.

This is the man who is content to be what he is, to evoke no more than the ordinary caliber of trials upon himself. The world envies him and strives to be like him. This man has achieved a liberation of the entity which the esotericist —along with the psychologist—calls the *personality*. The former, however, regards it as only a single "entity" or aspect in the whole subtle and complex nature of man. The integrated man lives comfortably in his personality. If, in addition to this, he has achieved some accomplishments of an outstanding nature, then we are inclined to feel that he has savored the best of life. This man may be a business man or a professional; a scientist, minister, farmer, or artist. He may be a tradesman or laborer, for his choice of occupation has little bearing upon his state.

The difference between this man and the one who has begun the arduous process which leads to liberation is one of *faculty*. To make an analogy, consider a man living in a room with no windows who has so busied himself with the contents of his immediate environment that he is neither aware of the outside world nor has he ceased to find challenge and satisfaction with the immediate. But suppose he suddenly discovers the confines of his room. He inadvertently or deliberately creates a chink in the wall which surrounds him. Or, to put it more philosophically, his examination of the materials around him gradually leads him to infer a relationship between these and a reality beyond them. Depending upon the ardor of his heart and mind, he may be content just to enjoy the promise of this blossoming life. It is here we find a great number of people who have some small experience of mystical or religious awakening, and the sweet flavor of it is enough to brighten their lives to the end of their days. They finger and savor these intimate delights like children treasuring unexpected gifts, and they live on the promise of more to come in the after-life.

Not so the aspirant for liberation. His propensities are such and his will so abnormally strong that he must rapidly evoke all the trials attendant upon the destruction of the barrier which holds him from the universe of reality which he senses within and beyond his immediate environment. There has not been a religious teacher or philosopher throughout history of any stature who has not, in one way or another, alluded to the condition of man as though he were imprisoned. Some Christians tend to interpret this as the barrier which exists between life and death, or the life of earth and the life of heaven. But the teachers did not mean this. They were—in the fullest sense— "practical philosophers," men of faculty, and explorers—through direct experience—of a larger "environment" than any conceived of by the intellect. Then they tried to use words which would symbolize in a concrete way a state of imprisonment which is real enough, but difficult to describe because it has to do with psychic and psychological states of consciousness.

The word "spirituality" we will reserve for the experience of reality itself. No one can fully savor the realms of the spirit without first going through the arduous process which alone leads to an orderly and sustained experience of insight, with its accompanying satisfactions and burdens. And although the words "spirit" and "spirituality" are used with regularity and confidence, let us first earn faculty and some degree of clarity and access to reality before we talk about it. But notice the terse clues of the wise men of the past. There is a point where language leaves off and subjective experience begins, which accounts for the will-o'-the-wisp poetic phraseology of the sages. A real teacher teaches most by that which he declines to say.

Since it is a characteristic of our age that we are inclined to be extravagant with words, we hand out titles with such readiness that the revered words "teacher," "doctor," "philosopher" and "artist" are granted promiscuously to many who, in a pure sense, should surely not qualify. The vast majority of individuals whom we call teachers are technicians and specialists. There was a time when a differentiation was made between a philosopher and a layman —when it was publicly conceded that some men, by virtue of inborn gifts and the subsequent training of their faculties, were, in and of themselves, destined to give leadership. Scholars, statesmen, and craftsmen deferred to such as these. That is, they sought from such natural teachers a way of life and action that would elevate their own endeavors to a status of universal significance. The craftsman or technician did not abandon his skill, but he pursued it in proper relationship to his broader, spiritual aspirations. The teacher, in his turn, drew from nature and encouraged the recognition and cultivation of intuition in his subjects. Here was the natural flow of wisdom then: from nature herself, through the intuitions of the gifted, and hence to the layman of true aspiration, who completed the cycle, within his capacities, by learning to tune his own faculties to nature.

But such education has always been for the few, for at no time in our recorded history has civilization as a whole been ready for such education. To the practical philosopher, who works without relationship to psychological time, this fact is of relatively small consequence. He may deplore the state of things, but he accepts his work among the few; and he knows that his work is cumulative and is related to all similar endeavor, wherever and whenever it occurs. He also knows that such work is the leavening which protects humanity from the fate of spiritual oblivion.

There are degrees, then, of worthiness to be called "teacher." But such a word should at least include in its application to the individual the necessity for some philosophical qualification, be it nothing more than a high degree of sensitivity and a sense of values which transcends his immediate contribution. The artists, dramatists, and writers who have lifted the sights of men have, if only sporadically, become channels for intuitive insight. The spectator, if he happens to be apt, may experience a brief moment of revolution which alters his whole nature. The individual worthy of being called "teacher" is one, then, who has the capacity to inspire, to so subordinate himself to nature that under the stimulus of a teaching relationship, he regularly outreaches himself, and he readily finds the talent within himself to relate the immediate to the universal. Such individuals are certainly not common, but one meets them from time to time.

The majority of men and women of our age tend to regard the world scientifically and not philosophically. A scientific frame of mind leads to efficiency, but only a creative mind—whether artistic or philosophical—can break up the materials of life into their essences and renew the whole from the inside outward. It requires, again, some degree of faculty to enter the territory of the philosophers—a very real realm of living which is conditioned by the necessary psychic and psychological attributes for participation therein. If teachers and true philosophers are exceedingly rare, at least there are more individuals to be found with some talent for looking at things in a fresh and inspired way.

These are the hopefuls. They are more than that. They are the actual elements of "society according to nature," which is the only kind worth striving for. If we could gather them together some way, nourish and encourage them in the process that follows upon that first decisive discovery of the potency of the individual will, we would one day have navigators who could not mistake the way so badly. It is the man, the woman, and the child who must be reconstituted. All the rest of it is provisional. All of the deductions of the uninspired minds will introduce no fundamental answer to human problems, however highly "educated" they may be.

12. NEW SPECIES

THERE is a hopefully copious stream of people who are feeling a kind of collective intuition, as the giant machinery of modern education falters under the impact of agitations for reform. These people are not waiting for some authoritative guide to better education, for they have begun to look askance upon the whole institution-born hierarchy of opinion. Surely this needs to happen from time to time in any society, and the institutions themselves should be glad that they are not proof against the untrained but often lucid ideas that arise spontaneously from people who are stumbling along earnestly and in a fresh and pioneering spirit. As the history of education reveals, the innovations which leaven the standard practices of the institutions have often come from those who pursue an individualistic path.

Thus, in an unobtrusive but effective manner, individuals and families are merging their mutual dissatisfactions and searches via the means of collective efforts of one kind and another. Small, often well-written periodicals are springing up dealing with the pertinent questions of how children should be raised and educated, how people should best live to avoid the threat of materialism and hyper-scientism, what measures should be taken to bring about peace and better community relationships, and how man can make his philosophy or religion more purposeful. They are forming private schools, parent groups, and even communities to better implement their researches. Although one finds always, among explorers, some exaggerated types of personalities, these people are, for the most part, intelligent and courageous. In these educational efforts, one senses the groping, from various points of reference, for an avenue of access to the orderly center of life, to a hook-up with universalities.

We dare, therefore, to pursue the dream of philosophical education—a dream which is being experimented with and slowly realized in some quarters, in spite of the enormous problems in the way of it. We are after faculty—a growing and progressive or unfolding perception in the framework of which intellectual and technical skills will find a place, but will not be exalted to the position of first importance which they hold in an intellectual-scientific age.

The enormous preoccupation with skills and information which typifies most educational efforts is an unfortunate stress and leads directly away from the philosophical approach to life and learning. It is very difficult for the intellect which is uninspired by intuition to sense the vast reasonableness of the universe in which we move—to understand the subtle physics that bind the actor to his actions. The kindest act on the part of a child's guardian is to let go of his future, to deal so interestedly and creatively with the day in hand that the causes engendered cannot fail to yield good future consequences. But if the culture has such a hold upon us that we cannot view the child apart from that culture, our dedication to his welfare is only superficial. It has nothing to do with his soul's search—a search that ultimately has a highly practical function in the world we live in.

If, at this point, it now seems important to encourage children in the kind of education that leads to insight, we must look at some of the conditions that favor the acquisition of faculty. It is important that the adult participants see the necessity for the present thesis, and that each be devoted to his own search for awareness. Whenever awareness becomes arrested, accomplishment moves upon a lateral plane; if need be, endlessly. But the hour-to-hour digging and reaching, aspiring and examining, that break up this lateral movement is not easy. It requires a soul-racking steadfastness of purpose which in turn evolves a wise and fruitful technique. There must be a determined start in this process before one is ready to work with children toward the ends we have in view.

A life of intelligent discipline is indicated—one which offsets the current tendency toward a preoccupation with the intellectual and sensory gratifications. But the word "discipline" causes panic in a society which has so recently discovered the libido. A great deal of attention is given to this elusive part of man's nature which the esotericist sometimes calls "the desire nature" (and mysteriously but significantly treats as an entity), and the psychologists treat as a hidden part of man's consciousness. The therapist finds that man's psychological disorders grow out of the frustration of his desires, and that mental and emotional health is restored when the pent-up aggressive force resulting from the frustration is released in some harmless way. Therapy is ameliorative and reconciliatory, as it needs to be in the case of a sick person. It may lead to balance and adjustment within the framework of present-day society, and this is perhaps enough. It cannot, of course, liberate in the sense that we have used the word. So it is unfortunate that so many people consciously or unconsciously draw implications from therapy procedures to use as prophylaxis for themselves and their children. Child guidance generally has become ameliorative, largely out of respect for the havoc that can be wrought through repressed desires; but mostly because as a society, we are still struggling to understand ourselves.

With a whole change in emphasis, with a life sensitively cued to the Intelligence that issues from every quarter, one slips quite naturally into an aspect of his own consciousness where the troublesome desire nature can find little quarter. The practical philosopher does not exert himself in an effort to discipline, once he has taken the first steps. He listens acutely because he wants to hear; he walks quietly so that he may observe; he eats little so that his senses will be alert. It is his aspirations which force him to conform—a conformity he gladly makes for the joy of the rewards. Then it is the conditions of learning insisted upon by nature herself (we might say, "the nature of things") which train or punish him, as the case may be. And as he relates to children, he will direct them to the rewards which an inquiring life reveals, and their own conformity to the "rules" will be natural and not arbitrary. For the rest of it, discipline and the most significant aspects of education itself grow out of relationship.

His knowledge will never permit the philosopher to lead a child into selfish attitudes of mind and behavior, but it does not make a disciplinarian *per se* out of him either—even when he knows, beyond the shadow of a doubt, that the realms of the spirit are forever closed to the person of egocentric motive and undisciplined conduct. He trains, not by acting from without and imposing upon the child arbitrarily, but by being himself, his inspired self—that entity who is sensitively aware of all the ingredients of a situation, the overt and the hidden. Any child is challenged by an intelligent, conscientious adult to accommodate his behavior so that he may place himself in communication with the adult. If a child is exploiting such an adult, the adult will protest. At best, the protest will be dignified, but it will be forthright and firm. He will protest not because he feels insulted or imposed upon, but simply because communication cannot take place between two human beings in the atmosphere of the motive of exploitation. Communication is obviously essential to constructive relationship and cooperative work. Thus, nature ("the nature of things") imposes psychological limitations upon the conduct of those who aspire to live well—a fact which is the very basis for moral education.

Education that leads to insight must necessarily proceed first of all upon a moral basis, morality—intelligently understood—providing the only suitable rationale for physical and mental training. Eventually, among strong-willed, sensitive children and adults who are sufficiently interested to "play the game," a mysterious yet perfectly tangible change begins to take place. The self-interested focus which is characteristic of the imprisoning desire-nature beings to shift its center of gravity, so to speak. The individuals become truth-oriented, which means actually that they become humanity-oriented.

Observe, now, that in this vastly significant way of relationship, we are no longer fiddling with the personal desire-nature—the focal center of all analytic procedures; we are no longer placating and fearing its retaliation in the form of neuroses and psychoses. We have, instead, called upon an aspect of consciousness, in both child and adult, which is fully capable of dealing with its own problems. This is easier to write down than it is to practice, certainly, but it is a sure clue to personal freedom.

The question of the environment of learning arises next, and this will of course be a variable factor; for there are stages and "stations" along the way. Each requires something of a leap away from the well-worn grooves of common thought and practice, and each is good in so far as it achieves this honestly and without flamboyance. Wherever practical, however, the need for an environment of nature for best results is generally agreed upon. It has already been suggested that nature is the teacher—nature in its myriad aspects, nature in the fields and woods and in the deep recesses of the consciousness of man. This is not a sentimental or poetic observation, but a matter of fact to the sensitive awareness.

The mature philosopher is largely independent of environment and may pursue his work where he finds it. Not so the beginner, who must first gain sensitivity and perspective, which is to say, faculty. If this is not altogether impossible in present-day urban society, it is at least very difficult. Access to nature is one important aspect of the matter; but equally important for the serious student of philosophy and for children is the discovery of an environment which is not a projection of the psychological limitations of the prevailing culture. If man generally fails to achieve any marked degree of intuitive

awareness, then it may not be sought in the general thorough-
fares but rather in special byways. The pursuit of truth is no
less a science than any other type of research and, like the rest,
requires its "laboratory conditions." Insulation, not isolation,
then becomes necessary. Insulation is the wise selection of
environmental conditions — for training purposes only —
which give every advantage to the growing intuition.

A child placed in a natural, wisely-insulated environment
is in such an apt conditon for learning — for the wondrous
"unraveling" of himself and the universe about him — that
the guardian becomes merely an alert monitor. That is, he
may, by sensitizing his own observation, follow the clues
which arise naturally in the life of such a child which lead
him through a logical sequence of unfoldment; and by ex-
panding here, interpreting there, and by assisting with the
skills *as they arise*, lead the child toward such unpredictable
goals as are contained in his own perceptive regions. A life
creatively lived — not just busily, but with probing sensitivity — begets its own significant consequences. A wise young
man or woman who is well-grounded in the universalities
that a philosophically-oriented life teaches is proof against
any cultural situation. He finds his own goals and occupations and these are not likely to be trivial.

A certain analogy comes to mind at this point — a theatrical
presentation which opens in darkness and the scene is gradually revealed by spotlights thrown at one point and then
another, until the whole emerges meaningfully. Human
growth is like this — not consecutive in the sense of proceeding in a straight line, but coming "alight" from within in the
various areas of the inner and outer consciousness that work
toward a perfectly timed merging. Maturity is a point of
merging, and maturity itself is an ever-flowering condition.
The mind cannot foresee the pattern which the entity will
take in its full-flowering state, but the intuition may find
recurring hints and suggestions along the way. The only
conceivable action is that which seizes the moment at hand
and wrings it dry of its meaning. This is what is meant by
dynamic relationships, and it requires intensive participa-

tion; a thing natural to children but more difficult for badly "educated" adults.

A child finds himself by the constant weighing of himself in relationship to his guardians. He grows "through" the adults in whom he has come to have confidence and respect; and when he is ready to try his own weight, he pushes away. His readiness for life will depend upon the moment to moment worth of his relationships. If these have been trivial or unhealthy, he will never awaken, never become educated. If they have been wisely instrumented, Intelligence will have found a place of operation, and he will have come into his own natural inheritance. In a word, he will be educated.

13. THE FIELDS BEYOND

AT THIS point, there is probably a burning question in the mind of the reader which may be stated in this way: "All right —given this family which has stepped out of the common run of things and devoted itself to the intuitive life, how does it relate back to the community and to the world?" It would seem that there is a sudden lacuna in the plan of nature, but this can hardly be so. We return to the same principles about which we have been talking right along and extend them a bit further.

In the same way that an individual reacts upon his family and environment under the impulse of intuition—ending up with the few who have the stamina and insight to go along with him as wife, friend or whatever—so the family itself acts upon the community about it and the world at large. It is no idle thing that this independent family has undertaken. It has, by its determination to act only in accord with the soundest and most far-reaching principles of life, attracted to itself advancing forces of evolution. It has made itself amenable and responsive to these forces, and so it is not in any sense alone. In spite of the world-wide tendency to vacillate in matters of personal integrity, and to follow the line of least resistance, there is hardly a person who does not feel a certain grudging respect for the "individualist" (if he is a sincere, intelligent person and not just a sensationalist). It is because his instincts tell him that here is a man who is representative of something bigger than himself.

Our intuitive family, then, sets up its own peculiar attracting forces, and equally strong repelling forces. Its associates become those who find some affinity with its views and ways, and a common relationship springs into being. The collective influence of a body of earnest individuals who qualitatively—if not quantitatively—are of the caliber to exert a subtle but inexorable shaping influence upon the destiny of mankind is something to think about. It may be a strong incentive to the ones who are on the borderline between intellect and intuition, who are weary of the old but timid of the new.

In order to relate to the community and to society as a whole in a meaningful way, one must be selfless and conscious of the silent workings of nature through every living thing. How can one cooperate with the positive intent of evolution if there are social preferences and aversions? Yet all of our popular forms of social exchange are based upon a pleasure-seeking principle. We tend to seek the people who make us feel most comfortable. We speak of liking those with whom we have "things in common," but usually, this means only that they do not challenge us in any uncomfortable way—that they assist us in our desire for self-approval and security.

When we let go of our attachments and our restless search for approval and affection from others, we see another concept of relationship which is constructive and purposeful. Among enlightened people, life would become like a great madrigal—a large pattern of movement which has rhythm and significance when properly understood. At certain appointed moments in the rhythm and exchange of partners, one pauses briefly before another who has turned up in front of him, and there is a swift, intensive exchange. But then the music changes again, and the relationship terminates in the onward flow of movement. There is no regret, for other moments are to come with the same or other persons as partners. Besides, if one were to suddenly turn pettish and decide that one person was better than another to be with, he would obviously throw the whole rhythmic pattern into confusion.

A detached person will soon discover that his relationships have a deep and profound meaning. If he is free of the desire to manipulate these exchanges, but instead, permits the ingredients in himself and the other an opportunity to interact, then he will discover those with whom he has "legitimate business." Very little in the life of the intuitionist is haphazard and meaningless. The smallest moments, the briefest contacts may have deep significance. But when personal desire colors relationships, then nature cannot act. In the long run, the process of natural selection will prove the most satisfying as well as the most beneficial. Purely social relationships give way to relationships of expediency and mutual welfare.

A group that draws together automatically through conscious or unconscious affinity of purpose becomes *ensouled*. A pervading purpose and spirit move the group itself and its various parts. There is no overlapping of function, no competition, no greater or lesser, no leader or persons being led. No one person can know better than the rest because each unit lends its unique voice and shape to the whole body, and it does so from hour to hour, so that the condition of things is always fresh—the challenge unpremeditated, the goals unthought-out. Cooperation is an intelligent functioning of the concept of *laissez faire*—a thorough conviction that nobody can get there unless everybody gets there. And that "there" is nowhere but "here" . . . in the full, rich living of the present moment as an individual, as a couple, a family, a society, a world. Cooperation cannot be planned. It is the spontaneous result of each person's being true to the highest in himself. It is the efflux of selfless behavior.

Long it may be before the world is ready for such cooperation, yet each individual who learns to trust his intuition and to encourage its voice in his affairs is a potential member of a new kind of community and society. If the principle of right relationship is clearly recognized, then there remains only to give it sufficient practice. Clumsily, imperfectly, forgetting sometimes the new feel of things, intuitive people are laboring to create a new world, for the one that now exists is not of nature, but of erring and recalcitrant mankind.

*   *   *

At times when you are very quiet and when desire and emotion have become stilled, you can observe the quiet shaping of yourself from within—can see the form you are intended to take, the work you should do—your function in the environment and the scheme of things. It is very important to see this. This is not forecasting as the astrologers and soothsayers do it; it is a deep and intelligent observation of your own nature and propensities. When you have seen yourself clearly, then it stops all the speculation and striving, all the doubt and uncertainty. It puts an end to ambition. In the rarified atmosphere of truth, your words, your thoughts, your acts will bring manifest form to that quiet vision; and it matters not what slothful, ugly and insane influences are abroad in the world.

So much of man's striving is simply to see himself clearly and to interpret the promptings of his own destiny. That destiny may be read in your likes and dislikes, your desires and aptitudes, your strengths and weaknesses. Every life presents a graph in which the destiny may be read. What you *might* be may be delicately sorted out from the mess of complacency and self-deceit. It may be warmed and succored by the breath of intuition and made impervious to the evil winds that would coax it into bland and stupid oblivion.

Afterword

THE TRAVELER IN WINTER

BY THE time this edition is in print, I will be nearing the age of
seventy, so a very natural question arises: How has the
process described in this book affected my life? I have been
looking at that question during recent weeks. At first my
mind roved over the many and varied events in the past—the
travels and occupations, the several countries where I have
lived, and the interaction with groups and individuals of a
number of nationalities, ethnic origins, and life styles. Much
of this was colorful and dramatic. Often it was sad.

But curiously, it has no place in terms of what I want to
examine here. From my present perspective, snipits of the
past look like a basketful of odd mementos and curios, interesting in their way, but quite lifeless, quite desiccated. I'm
glad that I was able to draw meaning from them and then let
them go.

Seniorhood presents itself to me as an extraordinarily
potent and busy time. There are periods in our lives when we
are especially aware of the hand of nature at work in our
bodies and senses. Adolescence is one such time; pregnancy
another. The "mid-life crisis" also presents challenges and

changes. But few of us are prepared to meet old age and death. In the natural course of life (how sad that there is so little left that *is* natural!) there would be much to engage and enthrall the elderly. One's senses feel a heightened activity, like the scurrying and rustling of forest creatures who foresee, without dread, the coming of winter. There are hints, intuitive whisperings, sudden moments of flashing perspective. Even the diminishing physical capabilities are not to be lamented, but are rather a divestment appropriate to the spare, light journey ahead.

So I patiently contain my former follies and impetuosities in their resultant effects upon my aging body because, beneath all of this, there is "the good death" about which I have written and spoken so much. It is composed of many little deaths along the way, when flashes of insight bring about fundamental transformations that alter the course of one's life. It commences with the inner life, and its effects become out-pictured in practical life.

But when and how did I first realize the finality of physical death? I believe it was when, as a child, I attended the funeral of my great aunt. My impression was that wherever my great aunt might be, she certainly wasn't in that shriveled doll-like object in the casket. I felt no fear nor grief.

The second impression was of the line-up of elderly people who passed by the casket, pausing for a moment to peer down timorously, then moving on by with faces that were un-informed, bewildered, and frightened. Seeing them thus, near the end of their own lives, my chest tightened and small popping sobs got loose and embarrassed me. They were sounds of frustration and anger. Why could not these people who had lived so long tell me anything about death? How could I find out?

Some years later, I saw what I must do. I must never run away psychologically. I must confront head on everything that confused or frightened me, because I sensed that the only real understanding or resolution lay right through the center of the matter—the heart of the flame. *That* I must approach without desire for a given result or reward. None of the old investigative ways of the mind would do. I needed access to the new, the untried, a wholly different quality of observation and learning. This came as an overwhelming realization.

At this point, I began to have a recurring dream. I was facing a tunnel of flame. A gentle companion urged me not to turn back, to walk with confidence on through the fiery center. I would peer into the heart of flame and see that there was a quiet opening like the eye of a storm. Then I would wake up.

How could I walk through the flame without looking back? I felt it meant living without choosing, without preferences or aversions, without imposing my ideas. Instead of choosing, I learned to scan, to sense, to track. Or I would reason as far as reason would take me, then leave it to "work," like yeast, before moving on. Although seeking no result, I came to discover that whenever I touched a bedrock of truth by the means described, it made an indelible mark. Later, it seemed that these scratchings were growing into some sort of beachhead on a new frontier. I was learning the feel, the silent language, the natural laws governing a terrain quite different from that of this world.

However incomplete my beachhead (and it appears to be very incomplete), it is real to me. Sometimes I see it as the dark markings on a space map where the needle indicates, "Here are signs of life. Someone has been here and left something to build upon." It was time, I felt, to start recording in writing the process by means of which I was making my discoveries.

To adhere to untried ways—to stubbornly set my compass by sightings in the regions of the inner senses—has cost me all of the shocks and upheavals that the younger traveler predicted. Husband and wife were finally torn apart by diverging values, and harsh changes altered the course of a number of lives. Once one has yielded totally to the process, there is no return. For to go on doing that which contradicts one's intuitive perception of truth is to invite illness and mental confusion.

But first there were the years of getting the feel of the inner faculties. Looking back, it is as though I lived much of my life with part of my attention fixed upon an inner aperture through which I have threaded the contents of my days and nights. The culling brought two matters under special focus. The first is the question of the uses and abuses of authority; the other is the function of will power in creative awareness. I had never been sure how to handle these two critical and inter-related forces, for that is what they are. Then recently while I was sorting out my files, I ran across some random writings pertaining to these very issues.

The material was penned during the rebellious sixties while I was living in La Paz, Mexico. The pages lay among other pieces on various subjects that were not necessarily meant for publication. Now here they were—a bit yellowed, fastened with a rusty clip, and smelling of the sea waters off the coast of Baja. They are evidence that the two subjects of authority and will power already had a hold on me; even then they in-fused my total awareness and evoked a perception so strong and undeniable that it became the rock upon which my marriage and career eventually foundered. I was sixty years old when full clarity came, and it took enormous resolve to start over again so late in life.

The pages from the past seem to have been waiting for this point in time, so I record them here:

I find I can scarcely sort out from the inner tangle of my thought and feeling the truth about the problem of authority. This truth taps me on the shoulder like a gentle ghost who is not too impatient but who wishes to make his point all the same. My past conditioning cringes under his touch, and I am at one moment rooting on the side of the anti-establishment people and then dashing cross the bleachers to side with the reactionaries. This is the difficulty, of course—this tendency of the mind to see things in black or white or gradations thereof. Actually the gradations—the so-called moderate positions—are all of the same fabric as the extremes.

The ghost is trying to get me to turn away from the mean problem and its meaner confines and to see something alto-gether different. I catch a glimpse of it, and I grieve over the abuses to which we submit our wondrously sensitive natures.

We are pliable and hopeful entities, capable of inner configurations of rare delicacy and impressionability. But the way of the mind is to seesaw on the grim scale of calculation and assessment. We have inherited, all of us, the fatal ways of the mind.

Strange . . . I am just now listening to a recording of Fauré's *Requiem* sung by a famous boys' choir. I hear again the angelic voice of the little boy soloist and wince with a chill intimation of something deadly out of which that pure perfection of tone and technique was born. A *requiem,* of all things! No child could sing so well without being placed under unnatural restraints that must handicap his access to the very heaven world toward which the music yearns. Perhaps only last year, before the child turned eight and came to choir school, he knew God a little. Unless he is very exceptional, he will probably have to content himself for the rest of his life with imitations of his early experience of God. It is probable, too, that he will become firmly ensconced in a secular worship.

Ah! The record has just finished and the music of Schumann and Brahms with adult voices has been dropped down by the player mechanism. These mature voices are giving me other sensations. What a relief! Just so. Discipline is appropriate for the adult choral group, whose members are old enough to understand the restraints inherent in any art form and are free to accept or reject them. But such restraints may very well prove crippling for a child. I cannot help it. I do distinctly feel this deadliness—the sacrifice of that inner freedom that opens the way to the life of the spirit.

The thing that the ghost is trying to tell me—and that my mind working in its monotonous pattern of oscillation struggles over—is to give up my sordid addiction to the traditional criteria for excellence. *Inner freedom and susceptibility is the treasure.* It is this condition that must not be endangered nor sacrificed; or, since it is bound to be lost once childhood forsakes us, it must be recovered. Nothing—absolutely nothing in the world or out of it—is more important.

So when does authority manifest in non-destructive ways? There is the voice of God, nature, or truth accessible to the intuitions of decent and intelligent people. There is the power of love and creativity that hums through a hive of bees and other collective organisms—the more so at levels where the intellect is inoperative. There are times of crisis when human beings work together without thought of self, when their instincts—purged by the common threat—work almost unconsciously for the collective welfare.

The next time a child is placed in my care or I am called upon to give an opinion affecting the welfare of myself, another, or a group of people, I shall try not to use my oscillating mind, not to support any side, any person or idea. I shall be especially wary of the impressive weight of my own years, experience, or judgment, for all are suspect. I will try to be a learning teacher.

I shall be as still as death and make a small, spot-lit area in the center of my being. I shall watch it and, by means of a passive will, arrest the movement of my conditioned memories, fears, and knowledge. It is possible if I watch very carefully that God may visit that quiet place. It is possible that truth may show a little of itself. I think this is what the ghost is trying to show me as he continues to tap me lightly on the shoulder.

It was very difficult to implement the insight of the quoted material and of the chapters in *The Process of Intuition* relating to educational philosophy. (They are, incidentally, my favorite chapters.) In the context of authority in which I struggled to work as a teacher, there were only limited opportunities to approach learning in the spirit that seemed right to me. I felt that authority must come from nature, and that to perceive it is to yield up all personal claim to it. Will power is an enforcer, and most of the folly in this world is created when great energy is applied to improperly perceived goals.

While living in the wake of consequences from the action I took to break with the past and start over, I put this question to a friend who practices psychiatry: "How is it that one can look at one's emotional trauma with deep objective insight—understanding the problem and its origin—yet continue to feel great pain?" He said, somewhat sardonically, "When you learn the answer to that question, will you please inform the people in my field?"

I don't presume to know the answer, but I continue to learn

some interesting facts about myself. During and following what my friend called the "holocaust" in my personal life, every instinct and intuition demanded that I stay *with* the pain, even as I had taught myself. I was amazed to find that I still had the psychological stamina for it, and that the unstinting inner observation did bring me, at last, through the flames and to a new-found freedom. It was another rebirth from one more "little death," and it proved more significant than any I had previously experienced.

I suggest that nature, by means of the process, seeks for each of us a comprehensive freedom beyond what I am able to describe. Any human problem is so profoundly linked to *all* human problems that one has to wonder if it may not be *our addiction to life as we live it on planet Earth* that is at the root of all of our misery. Why don't we change? Why don't we "die" to our addiction to selfishness and ambition, to greed, lust, and violence, and to many lesser but insidious proclivities, such as dependency, complacency, pride, and self-rightiousness? I know that there is one state of consciousness in which this collective pestilence thrives as germs thrive in stagnant water. There is another state in which they have no meaning at all—where they lack a favorable environment in which to generate. I don't mean some trance-like state of mind which permits a temporary escape and euphoria. We can't hop over our problems and abandon them.

I suggested that awareness must become comprehensive, and this demands dedicated attention to the smallest details of motive and action. What an enormous task this proves to be! Yet we must begin somewhere. How about a period each day during which we listen to our thoughts and words with curiosity and detachment; when we observe the ebb and flow of our feelings and emotions—especially in relation to others, but also to material objects and goals. Generally speaking, most of us are unacquainted with ourselves and the ways in which the deeper levels of mind function. We are involved with an image rather than an actuality.

Freedom as our forefathers put it is something that we pursue. I would go further and say it is a vocation above and beyond all other occupations and professions. When one sees a truth not just intellectually but with the clarity of intuition, that truth spontaneously translates into action. When you or I change to any degree, this change affects the whole of humanity.

The Process of Intuition has been, for me, a touchstone to the life of the spirit during those mortal moments we all experience, when mind and flesh hold us too tightly and we feel disoriented and forsaken. Letters I have received from various parts of the world (even from a man in prison) report similar experiences. One woman wrote recently, "This book spoke to my own personal need at the very time I was reaching for something." This collective evidence underscores our oneness and the universality of both the need and the cure we seek in our common search for freedom.

THE PROCESS CONTINUES IN OTHER QUEST TITLES

THE ENLIGHTENED SOCIETY by John L. Hill
A study and forecast of society's developing spiritual awareness.

THE FAMILY UNCONSCIOUS by E. Bruce Taub-Bynum
The unconscious levels of communication inherent in the family and their effect.

SPIRALS OF GROWTH by Dwight Johnson
The ascent of the spiral path that leads to the realm of superconsciousness.

THEATRE OF THE MIND by Henryk Skolimowski
From instinct to intuition. Our developing awareness based on an ever-growing sensitivity to life.

Send for our complete catalog:
Quest Books
306 W. Geneva Road
Wheaton, IL 60187